PRAISE FOR

FALLING DOWN TO FIND MYSELF

"It's not too often that you get a chance to take a deep dive into the full story of a friend that you think you already know. Kevin and I met as SlamBall teammates, and on top of being a great teammate, he is an absolute warrior! We have been able to remain in touch over the last almost-twenty years, but *Falling Down to Find Myself* gave me not only a deeper insight to Kevin, but a deeper appreciation for the person that he is, what he has overcome, and how he plans to serve and inspire others with his story. While this book reads like we are sitting around a campfire, with Kevin sharing story after story with us, you realize that you are celebrating failures just as much as victories with him, while you learn along the way. Digging into the 'Who vs. What' forces a positive introspection and politely demands action and the 'Will to W.I.N.'"

—TREVOR [T.A.] ANDERSON, CSCS, speaker, educator, coach, performance specialist, owner/creator of Better Every Day, and former professional SlamBall and football player

"Kevin's story is brimming with a blue collar wisdom that's been learned and earned by someone who has persevered through life ever since taking his first breath. This book shines a light on the philosophy needed to navigate adversity with Kevin's own brand of stick-to-itiveness and 'burn the ships' mentality that helped him attain his highest aspirations regardless of what life threw at him. In essence: words from a guy who lived it."

—DEVAN LONG, former NFL player and current actor

"As one of the guys on the receiving end of that drop kick, I can attest to how hard-hitting Kevin and this book are."

—CHRIS GIZZI, strength and conditioning coordinator for the Green Bay Packers and former NFL player

"Kevin has proven himself time and time again. This book is only a snapshot of the man he grew to become. Kevin has proven that if you believe in yourself and apply what you know, then you can achieve pretty much anything. He took time to reflect on what it means to be a good man. Reading this book has not only inspired me but continues to lead me. This is not a one-time read but something that we all can relate to. No one is perfect but we all have to try! I would recommend this book not as a testimony but a simple guide that maybe we all could use . . . Never give up!"

—RENFORD LIGON, Airborne Ranger, Task Force 160th, Special Forces (Green Beret), author, actor, stuntman, mentor, friend

"*Falling Down to Find Myself* is such a testament to Kevin's perseverance, mental philosophy, and individual growth through the challenges of life's ups and downs. What a great go-to memoir!"

—TRACY BENNETT, former NFL kicker, photographer, twenty-year veteran of the movie industry, and entrepreneur

HOW A HOLLYWOOD STUNTMAN CONQUERED LIFE'S BUMPS AND BRUISES TO CULTIVATE A PHILOSOPHY FOR TRUE HAPPINESS

FALLING DOWN TO FIND MYSELF

KEVIN CASSIDY

RIVER GROVE
BOOKS

This book is a memoir reflecting the author's present recollections of experiences over time. Its story and its words are the author's alone. Some details and characteristics may be changed, some events may be compressed, and some dialogue may be recreated.

Published by River Grove Books
Austin, TX
www.rivergrovebooks.com

Distributed by River Grove Books

Design and composition by Greenleaf Book Group
Cover design by Greenleaf Book Group
Cover Image: ©Shutterstock/G-Stock Studio

Publisher's Cataloging-in-Publication data is available.

Print ISBN: 978-1-63299-584-1

eBook ISBN: 978-1-63299-585-8

First Edition

For everyone who helped me maintain my bearings.

The most terrifying thing is to accept
oneself completely.

—CARL JUNG

CONTENTS

PREFACE

Self-knowledge is no guarantee of happiness, but it is on the side of happiness and can supply the courage to fight for it.

—SIMONE DE BEAUVOIR

"GOOD MORNING, CASS," said the man with the clipboard.

"Good morning, Coach," I replied, feeling slightly odd calling this guy "Coach." He wasn't really a coach, but I was in a football locker room suiting up for contact and he was my boss, so "Coach" it was. Looking around the room, I saw that I was surrounded by football talent far superior to my own. Former NFL players and guys who had just finished playing at the University of Southern California, the University of Texas, Texas A&M, UCLA, and Cal Berkeley were suiting up alongside me. I was twenty-four years old, in decent shape, and standing at 6'3" and 230 pounds, I seemed to fit right in. At least physically. The problem was that I hadn't put on a helmet since high school and although back then I had the opportunity to play in college, I never did. For some reason however I was strangely confident running out onto the field with these other guys. Why? Good question. It's because this wasn't real football. It was movie football. I was on the set of *The Longest Yard*, the remake with

Adam Sandler and Burt Reynolds. It was my first movie job, and I was stoked. Running onto the field that day, I never would have guessed that my actions would result in one of the most memorable hits in the movie and be featured in the trailer of my very first film.

That I was cast in this role at all is kind of miraculous. Months before, back in Los Angeles, I went to a tryout with the goal of being hired to perform the football action in the movie. This was a private tryout as opposed to a public casting call, so even being invited to attend was a pretty big deal. The first step was to show up at an auditorium with thousands of other people, fill out a questionnaire, and wait in line to talk to the "coach" to see if you were good enough on paper to lace up the cleats the following week at the tryout. This was a different world than any other I had been involved in my previous twenty-four years on this earth. LA was a different beast and this formerly bullied, deformed kid from the East Coast who looked a little funny and talked even funnier was out of his league . . . or so I thought.

In a story I'll elaborate on later, a year or so prior to this tryout I was playing professional SlamBall, full contact basketball played on a court with trampolines. It was on TV for a few years in the early 2000s. I was one of the best players at my position and odds are if you were up at one o'clock in the morning watching SlamBall on Spike TV all those years ago, I was on your screen. Turns out the "coach" doing the hiring for *The Longest Yard* had been a SlamBall coach prior to my arrival in the sport. He saw SlamBall on my resume and immediately handed me an invitation to the tryout without noticing my lack of high-level football experience. At the tryout the following week—which was run similarly to the NFL Scouting Combine—I didn't blow the coach away with my talent, but I didn't embarrass myself either. I am very athletic, and I held my own, but no way was I going to make the team on that basis alone. I was going to need fate to intervene on my behalf . . . and it did.

I found out later that I was chosen for the movie not because of my football skills, but because someone from my past had recommended me based on my work ethic and character. This person was the coach's assistant, a woman who was involved in SlamBall at the same time I was. She'd seen me working day in and day out and witnessed my athletic ability. But more than that she knew I was on time every day and that I was a great teammate. I was smart, hard-working, coachable, and followed directions. She had been involved in casting football movies in the past and knew that these skills were as important as the on-field tryout results. So, when it came time to choose the football talent for this movie, she stood up and personally vouched for me. I may have been graded a C in the Combine but I had earned an A in Character, and this woman put her job on the line for me. I am eternally grateful to her, as her faith in me changed the course of my life.

More to come on what transpired following that run out of the locker room and onto the set of *The Longest Yard* that day, but I don't want to get ahead of myself. This book, much like life, is not about the destination—it's about the journey.

The journey that landed me on this movie set was a long and arduous one even before the tryout. Before I moved to LA, before I began my teaching career in Baltimore, before moving from New York to North Carolina as a kid, and honestly before I can even remember. What I learned throughout my many life experiences that got me there and beyond is the motivation for this book. I have been many things throughout my journey and have played different parts in the play that is life. I have grown, matured, failed, and succeeded along the way and like most evolved humans, I have become a different person because of it. Different for sure, but the same in so many ways. After all, I am the same person, right? Or am I? There's a philosophical rabbit hole if I ever saw one!! This question of *who am I* and *when do I become something or someone new, if I ever really do*, has always intrigued me. The ancient Greek philosopher Heraclitus said this on the topic: "No man ever steps in the same river twice for it's not the same river and he's not the same man." Profound, and in my opinion true. Throughout my life I've pondered this in a way that was distracting. A type of daydream I found myself chronically drifting into. That daydream always led to the same question though: *when* does the man become a different person and at what point can we define the river as new?

This nagging search for a pleasing answer to this question coupled with a life spent having to change into another person time and time again ultimately led me to writing this book. Thankfully, I was able to satisfy my philosophical need for an answer. The answer that brought closure to my busy mind on the topic involves another philosophical paradox called The Ship of Theseus and a personal philosophy that's been trapped in my brain for years that I call *Who vs. What*. These two thought experiments violently collided, and the resulting byproduct was peace of mind and an end to the recurring daydream.

I believe I've stumbled onto something that can help people find their way to a happier, more confident, and fulfilling life, and I'm eager to tell the world about it. The Who vs. What question and The Ship of Theseus Paradox helped me decipher my own life experiences in such a way that I was finally able to understand how I managed to come out on top at the end of the day . . . as well as realize there are many more days yet to come.

As I share my life's story in the pages that follow, I will ask myself the Who vs. What question many times and use my life as a personification of The Ship of Theseus. It's going to be a wild, fun, sad, and exciting ride. A ride that will take you from a movie set to a jail cell, to a stadium full of screaming fans, to a couch in a friend's living room. At the end of the ride you will have gotten to know me a lot better, but more importantly, hopefully you will have gotten to know yourself on a higher level. If you're a young person trying to understand yourself and your place in the world, this book is for you. If you're a person in some sort of transition (heading to college, dealing with grief or a serious illness, in between jobs, coming off a relationship, an empty nester), this book is for you, too. It's also for people—parents, grandparents, neighbors, educators, coaches—who know a young person or any person making a transition and want to help them face their challenges with humble confidence.

Humble confidence. That's what it's all about . . . that's what having a good grip on who you are creates. Confidence without humility is just ego, and "Ego Is the Enemy," as author Ryan Holiday so starkly puts it.[1] If my book helps you have humble confidence in *Who* you are, not *What* you are (a concept I will dive into very shortly), it will be worth the seventeen years I spent falling down stairs in movies and all the years prior to that when I was getting bullied, beaten up, and called "Rat Boy" at school.

CONFIDENCE WITHOUT HUMILITY IS JUST EGO.

I will tell you all about it . . . But first let's explore Who vs. What and unpack The Ship of Theseus Paradox. I encourage you to think deeply about these philosophies as I explain them and see how you have personified them in your own life. As I elaborate on these topics in the introduction leading up to my life story, I will use examples from my

1 Holiday, Ryan. *Ego Is the Enemy* (New York: Portfolio, 2016).

stunt career that involve some of the biggest movie stars in the world, and I promise to make it fun and informative. Consider this the warmup before a big workout. This warmup will ensure you are maximizing this book's potential.

INTRODUCTION

WHO VS. WHAT

IF I ASKED YOU, "*WHO* ARE YOU?" what would your answer be? If I then asked, "*What* are you?" would your answer be the same or would it change? Who are you and What are you? Take some time to answer those two questions for yourself. Put the book down and really think about the difference between these two things. Maybe you think they are one and the same and that's fine. Like most philosophical questions, there are no wrong answers. We each get to respond and rationalize in our own way.

For me, differentiating my Who from my What—or even realizing that there was a difference, then further realizing that that difference was hugely relevant to my attitude and future success in life—took a lot of mental anguish and did not come quickly. My first answer to "What am I?" was "I am a human being." Maybe I'd just watched a sci-fi movie or something, but this seemed like the most logical response at the time. But then I pressed myself to take it a step further. *Okay, I'm a human being . . . what else*? Well, I'm a son, a brother, a father, a husband; I am tall, strong; I was a bullied child with a severe birth defect; I was a standout athlete, a middle-school teacher, a Hollywood stuntman, and now an entrepreneur and an author, and in between I was . . . everything in-between, I guess.

Next, I asked myself the Who question. "Who am I?" The answer: I am Kevin Cassidy. *Yep, obviously. But keep going.* At first, I just recycled the Whats but I wasn't satisfied with that. I was stuck.

Then I realized that the Who is something different. It's something that has been there through all the Whats but it's deeper, less tangible. Kevin Cassidy is the Who, but who the hell is that? This is where the snowball built up momentum and really started rolling down the hill. Who I am is confident, honest, hard-working, scared, smart, unsure, unworthy, fair, and a myriad of other personality traits and values that mature and evolve over time. Who I am is the complex personality traits, the sense of morality, the never perfect but always improving individual that grew and evolved over time and has been present through all the Whats I had become. What I was may have changed three times in as many months (e.g., football player to baseball player, bullied kid to popular kid, etc. . . .) while the Who has only slowly evolved during that time, if it has changed at all.

What I was at one point in my life was a high school athlete. Who I was at that same point was an aggressive, loving, hard-nosed, honest kid who thought he'd live forever.

Knowing the difference between your Who and your What is one thing, but prioritizing them properly is the light that shines the way to a happier future. Ultimately that is the goal and focal point of this book. It is easy—pretty much our default—to prioritize the What in our lives and we must do that to some extent. But that What will crumble under its own weight if the Who isn't strong enough to support it. Going back to *The Longest Yard* tryout . . . I was able to get on the field and try out because of a What in my life (having been a SlamBall player), but I made the team because of my Who (the intangibles the coach's assistant saw in me during SlamBall).

KNOWING THE DIFFERENCE BETWEEN YOUR WHO AND YOUR WHAT IS ONE THING, BUT PRIORITIZING THEM PROPERLY IS THE LIGHT THAT SHINES THE WAY TO A HAPPIER FUTURE.

Let's explore this concept further through another story from my movie career involving one of the world's biggest stars . . .

THE ANGELINA EFFECT

Generally speaking, I'm not the kind of guy who gets starstruck. My attitude has always been that no matter how "important" a person might be, people are people, plain and simple. But I have to admit that when I saw Angelina Jolie—*the* Angelina Jolie!—walking across the set to meet me on the first day of shooting our shared scene in the 2010 movie *Salt*, I felt a bit intimidated. To be honest, I had some preconceived notions about Angelina and they weren't all flattering. I expected her to be demanding, aloof, a diva. Like practically everyone else on the planet, I knew her resume well: she was Hollywood elite, a highly paid superstar, an Oscar winner, Brad Pitt's significant other, a global sex symbol, savior of kids in Africa . . . etcetera, etcetera. Her pedigree is super impressive no matter how you slice it, so it wouldn't have been surprising if she was a bit full of herself. Now I was only seconds away from not just meeting her but working intimately with her for the next two weeks, acting out an extremely physical fight scene for her next major film. I'm a big guy at 6'3, 230 pounds, but at only 5'7, Angelina has the presence of a giant and I was honestly a bit nervous to meet her.

Then I saw her warm smile and her extended hand and heard her sincere greeting, and my intimidation melted away.

Our scene was filmed on a boat moored in the Hudson River just off of New York City's Chelsea Piers. There were paparazzi on the other side of the street, hundreds of them every day, clambering for the best viewing position and shouting, "Where's Angelina? Where's AJ?" Some of them even followed me to my changing room asking me if I knew where she was and what she was doing. I'd say, "Hey, I'm just a stuntman. They hit me and I fall down, that's all I know." Even after hearing that, they wouldn't let up. It was annoying as hell. By the third day I thought that if Angelina came to work that day and was a total bitch, I wouldn't blame her. I don't see how anyone can put up with that constant harassment. Yet every day for two weeks, Angelina was an absolute professional, the nicest person to everybody on the set.

She was physically strong and tough, too. Because of the close-up nature of our scene, she had to perform the action herself. She was trained and coached by her stunt double who was standing by for support, but AJ herself was going to have to bring it physically in this scene and that is exactly what she did. Ours was a brutal, precisely choreographed scene that consisted of punching, gun fire, and slamming each other around on this boat. At the end of each take, after she'd "killed" me, she would reach down and help me to my feet. She was a class act. She knew everyone's name, treated everyone as an equal, and on top of that brought such a positive energy to the set you couldn't help but enjoy yourself. Who she was shined so brightly that all the Whats on her resume seemed irrelevant.

Just as there is more to Angelina Jolie than her obvious role as a famous actor, there is much more to all of us than the various roles we've played in our lives. This is the difference between our Who and our What and it forms the backbone of a philosophy I tried to articulate unsuccessfully for years. It felt like the obvious word that was sitting on the tip of my tongue but refused to come out. These two simple questions—Who am I? and What am I?—and the soon-to-be-elaborated-on Ship of Theseus were the keys to rescuing the thoughts trapped in my mind.

To drive the Who vs. What mentality home, let's go back to the set of *The Longest Yard* for one more example.

I was very fortunate to meet a variety of famous people on this project. I was even more fortunate that the atmosphere and general vibe of this set was very welcoming. It should come as no surprise that any movie set that is ultimately run by Adam Sandler and his production team would be a "happy" place to work. On this set I met famous actors like Sandler, Burt Reynolds, Cloris Leachman, William Fichtner, Terry Crews, and Chris Rock as well as famous athletes like Michael Irving, Bill Goldberg, Bob Sapp, Bill Romanowski, and Brian Bosworth among others. To say it was a surreal experience would be an understatement. A unique aspect of this movie, though I didn't know it at the time, was how closely the stunt performers had to interact with the actors on a regular basis. We were essentially on the same team. We had practice and meetings together, and often times interacted outside of the set in Santa Fe, New Mexico, where a large portion of the movie was filmed. During all of this I was able to get to know a lot of these people on a personal and professional level. Each of them impressed me in their own ways, and I couldn't find a bad word to say about anyone involved in that movie even if I tried. As I reflect on that experience and through the years of answering questions and talking about being on that movie set, one person seems to jump into my mind more than the others. Every one of the people I mentioned previously and everyone I didn't mention are living embodiments of my Who vs. What philosophy. Upon meeting and interacting with them, each one individually had a more impressive Who than all their Whats combined. However, the person I keep coming back to, the one that always tops the list when someone asks me, "who impressed you the most?" or "who stood out even in that crowd?" was the rapper and entrepreneur Nelly.

Upon meeting him I had no real expectations or preconceived notions like I did with Angelia Jolie, and it really didn't hit me that he was so impressive until months into filming. He was a soft-spoken guy on set, always smiling and working hard. I could tell he was taking it all in and really concentrating on his acting craft. In other words, he was very professional. He was also the embodiment of the term "humble confidence."

Throughout the months of filming I learned that he was the first minority owner of a NASCAR team (truck series, I think), was part owner of the Charlotte Bobcats NBA team, and has multiple philanthropic causes ranging from fighting hunger and leukemia to sending kids to college. But the personal story about him and his group "the St. Lunatics" is probably the most impressive.

The short version of the story is: He was offered a big music contract after the group found some local success in the St. Louis area. The catch was that *he* was given the contract—not his group. He declined at first, so as not to leave his friends and music collaborators behind. Later, at their behest, he agreed but with a clause that his second album would include everyone. He then, of course, blew up with his hit *Country Grammar*. When the time came to record the second album, he refused and was ready to walk away from the money and fame if the label didn't stand by their word and have album number two be from the St. Lunatics and not just Nelly. He demanded that his friends and the people who got him there were recognized and given their share of the fame and money. Though I wasn't there and didn't know him at that time, I can absolutely vouch for his character. I am confident he wasn't bluffing. This is indeed the person I interacted with on the set of *The Longest Yard*, who has left a lasting impression on me, and who has helped me, without knowing, to better articulate this Who vs. What philosophy of mine.

It's necessary to say that all the things I learned about Nelly came from other people. He never mentioned any of it to me personally. He just had fun every day, worked hard, and filled the set with his electrifying smile and personality. Great people don't talk about themselves—other people will do that for them.

With all the distractions available to Nelly, all the Whats he was juggling, and probably still is, all anyone cared about was how nice, honest, and hardworking he was. The fact that you were naturally in a better mood and energized by being around him made anything tangible he did seem small. Like Angelina, his Who dominated all of his Whats.

The goal of this book is to tap into whatever that intangible thing is. The thing that Angelina, Nelly, and so many other people have. To reverse engineer it and find out how to accomplish that in each of our lives. Nobody is perfect and that includes these two, but if your Who shines bright enough all your imperfections seem to be blurred in the background of the bigger picture that is you.

I hope you have a good grasp of the Who vs. What theme and can see how this mentality can strengthen your character. It's crazy to say, but it took me an awkwardly long time to be able to articulate and explain the Who vs. What mentality the way I just did. Only after I wove The Ship of Theseus Paradox into my ongoing exploration of Who vs. What was I able to understand it fully and explain it to others. Let's unravel the paradox now and find out how it ties into Who vs. What.

THE SHIP OF THESEUS

I've always been a better macro learner. Meaning: it is easier for me to make sense of bigger, more tangible things than smaller, less tangible ones. I learn better when I am able to touch something or visualize it in a clear manner. In high school I struggled with chemistry as I couldn't touch the elements and had a hard time visualizing the various bonds between them, but I excelled in physics. Physics was bigger, clearer, and it made sense to me. Being able to physically hold things and mentally visualize the process of something like projectile motion made perfect sense, and plugging that into equations seemed natural. I was unable to fully comprehend and articulate my Who vs. What philosophy because I felt stuck in an intangible "chemistry" mindset.

The Ship of Theseus was the physics. It was the macro, tangible visualization I needed to fully understand the philosophy I have been trying to articulate. It allowed me to reinforce, build upon, strengthen, and personify the Who vs. What philosophy so I could get it off the tip of my tongue and out into the world. Let's dive into it!

THE SHIP OF THESEUS PARADOX

Imagine that a ship has been built by the Greek hero Theseus. We'll call it the Ship of Theseus, but that's really not important. We could call it the Ship of Kevin, or the Ship of Emily, or the Ship of Carlos. The name doesn't matter. What matters is that Theseus built this ship for the purpose of crossing the sea to reach the New World. It was built from the finest parts: the sturdiest mast, the strongest planks of wood, the biggest and best oars, and the most glorious sails. At last, the day came when it set off on its long and arduous voyage. It would encounter many storms and rough seas and be knocked off track countless times, but over and over again it fought to regain its course. Along this difficult journey the ship suffered damage. First one plank had to be replaced and then another, and another. Then the mast broke and had to be replaced. Then the oars started breaking and had to be swapped out for new ones.

By the time the Ship of Theseus got all the way to the other side of the world, it had been completely rebuilt one plank, one oar, one mast at a time. Not one of its original parts remained. Now riddle me this: when this ship lands on the other shore, *is it still the Ship of Theseus*? Is it still the same ship that set sail from a distant land all those years before even though it retained none of its original parts? If you think the answer is "yes," why is that? What is it that still makes it the Ship of Theseus? If you think the answer is "no," at what point did it become a different ship? Was it when the first plank was replaced, or the second one, or . . . when? At what point did the ship's identity change?

To take this one step further, imagine that as the Ship of Theseus was making its way to the New World there was another ship following it. Every time the Ship of Theseus dropped off an old plank, oar, or mast, the trailing ship picked it up. By the time the Ship of Theseus reached its destination, the other ship behind it had built a *third* ship made out of all the original parts of the Ship of Theseus. Now this ship made from all the original parts of the Ship of Theseus and the original but rebuilt Ship of Theseus are moored next to each other off the coast of the New World. Which one is the real Ship of Theseus? The one that's made from all the original discarded parts, or the one that was replaced plank by plank by plank along the way?

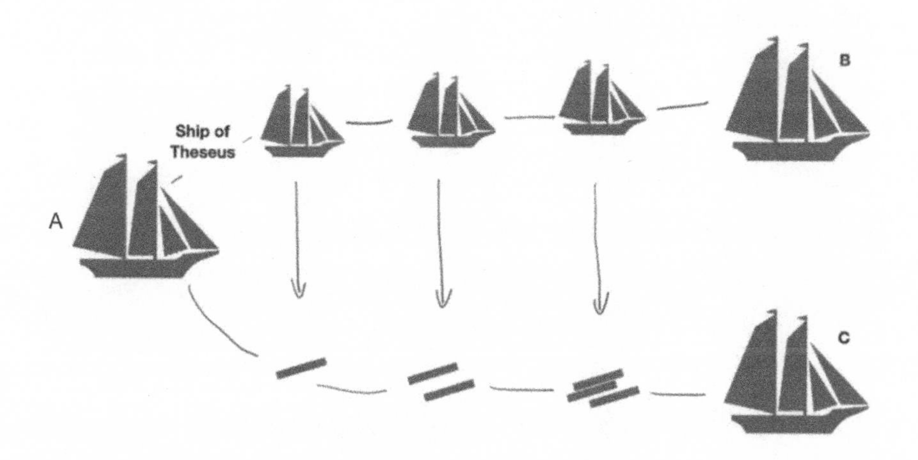

Just as with all paradoxes, there are no right or wrong answers here. Everyone gets to figure this out for themselves. However you want to interpret it to help yourself grow and increase your understanding of life is the correct answer. Five years from now, after having evolved and gained new experience, you might come to a different conclusion than the one you have today. It doesn't mean your answer now was wrong. It just means you may have different answers at different points in your life.

It hit me like a rock as I was pondering this paradox and Who vs. What. Every one of us is our own Ship of Theseus and each plank of our ship represents a What in our life. That was the missing piece, the visualization I needed. When I challenged this thought process over and over again, combining Who vs. What with this paradox in this way (we are the original Ship of Theseus and each plank represents a What) it continuously strengthened it. Throughout our journey of life across the sea we all encounter beautiful sunrises and dark storms and must at times replace planks and repair sails. If you refuse to make those repairs and replacements, your ship will never make it to the other side of the ocean. Just as if you as a person get wrapped up in a single What, e.g., baseball player, boyfriend, girlfriend, rich man, or poor man, your transition (and there's always a transition coming!) will be long and arduous. The longer you hold on to that identity and refuse to replace that plank, the longer you'll be drifting out to sea. Having your ship's identity completely wrapped up in any one plank instead of the purpose of the journey, and the humility to know you must evolve and adapt, causes that hopeless drift. The real-world result is you as a person never reaching your full potential. Maybe an even sadder byproduct is losing the ability to see the world as the beautifully mysterious place it is.

EVERY ONE OF US IS OUR OWN SHIP OF THESEUS AND EACH PLANK OF OUR SHIP REPRESENTS A WHAT IN OUR LIFE.

Think of the professional athlete who suffers a career-ending injury. If he or she has built their entire life around that sport to the exclusion of all else and that sport gets taken away suddenly, how well will they endure and how long will it take him or her to be "themselves" again? Think of the older man who gets laid off from the job he's had for forty years. That job was the number one thing in his life, but now it's gone. What's left for him if that's all he ever believed he was? It's a mistake to base your identity on any individual plank—a What—because that can, and probably will, change over time. But even if it doesn't (think religion, skin color, and sexual orientation) you'll lose objectivity, happiness, and a deeper sense of self if that What dominates your character and defines your Who instead of the other way around.

Even worse is the person whose identity is wrapped up in something negative. Take me, for instance. As you'll read in Chapter 1, I was born with a severe facial deformity and speech impediment that caused me to be bullied for the majority of my childhood. If I'd refused to constantly replace planks and just accepted that I was the "Deformed Bullied Kid," I would have had a pretty miserable life. The ability to not attach yourself to a What you find yourself in is a powerful weapon in life and a necessary one if you want to cultivate unshakable humble confidence and be truly happy. I see too many people identifying as one thing these days, unable to adapt and grow, and it breaks my heart. Maybe they weren't given the necessary tools early on in life, or they are enamored by the attention they receive from this one plank. The "why" doesn't matter. What matters is if they are able to see it or not and whether they are willing to evolve. Staying in this singular state of being poisons the human spirit. Many people have tied their complete Who to one plank on their ship like a pirate being held hostage and tied to the mast. In many cases these people are willing to go down with the ship, and some even think they are heroic for doing so. Even if this plank is the sturdiest and purest plank in the whole ship and doesn't need to be replaced, it takes the attention away from other aspects that may be falling apart. As a result, your ship will sink or be lost at sea and your Who will be drowned or lost along with it.

I'm hoping my life story in the pages that follow serves as a wakeup call for people who find themselves drifting out to sea. It's not impossible and it's never too late to regain control of your ship. Nothing about me is particularly impressive. I'm not as talented as Nelly or as beautiful as Angelina Jolie, but I was able to forge a similar mentality rooted in humble confidence. A mentality that enabled me to persevere, succeed, find happiness, and ultimately kept me in control of my ship. I hope you are able to do the same.

1

BORN WITH GRIT, JUST NOT A NOSE

When I was a little baby, I remember that one moment of calm peace, and three minutes after that, it was on.

—TUPAC SHAKUR

I'VE PLAYED A LOT OF BASEBALL in my life and been thrown more curveballs than I can count, but nothing compares to the curveball I was thrown on the day I was born. When I made my debut in the delivery room on that day in Long Island in 1977, the doctor immediately cut the umbilical cord, covered me with a towel, and dashed from the room carrying me like a football, marking the first of many times someone would look at me and wonder: *What the hell?*

I really can't blame him. He was the first person to see that I was born with a severe facial birth defect. Where the end of most people's nose is—where the nostrils should be—I had a bubble that extended past where my top lip should be and all the way back to my throat. Everything in between was hollow. There was nothing there. No roof of my mouth, no bone, and no place for baby teeth to grow. When the obstetrician ran from the delivery room with me in his arms, he carried me to the NICU where the neonatal team would spend the next few days keeping me alive and figuring out where to go from here. The official diagnosis came quickly: *orofacial cleft*, or cleft palate. The Centers for Disease Control estimates that every year in the United States 2,650 babies are born with cleft palate, so it's a fairly common birth defect.[2] Most of them aren't nearly as severe as mine was, though.

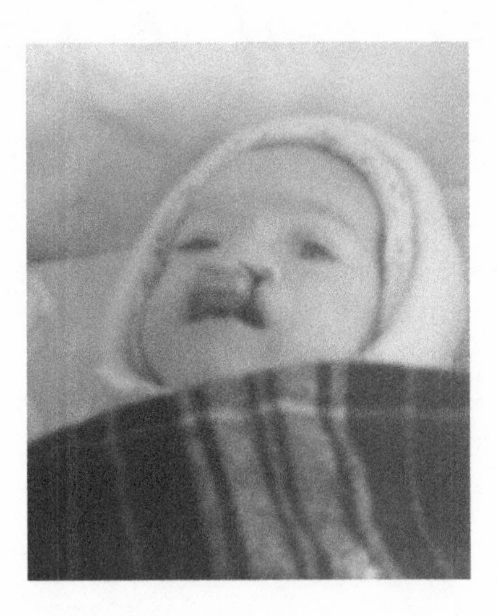

Naturally, my parents—my father, Tom, and my mother, Pat—were surprised by this unexpected plot twist. Back then they didn't have 3D ultrasounds and all the other prenatal tools we have now, so there was no way for anyone to know prior to my birth that I had such a deformity. My brother, Daniel, had been born strong and healthy just eighteen months before, but my parents had suffered the trauma of having a stillborn

---

2 SE Parker et al., "Updated National Birth Prevalence Estimates for Selected Birth Defects in the United States, 2004-2006," *Birth Defects Research (Part A): Clinical and Molecular Teratology* (2010) LXXXVIII, 1008-1016.

daughter prior to Daniel's birth. They were worried and confused (at the very least) when the delivery doctor immediately ran away with me.

Luckily, there happened to be a renowned cleft palate clinic at the hospital where I was born, so the medical team knew exactly what to do. A surgeon from that clinic, Dr. Harris, examined me in the NICU and went to talk to my parents before they were allowed to see me. He explained the diagnosis—my parents had no idea what a cleft palate was—and showed them a series of before-and-after photos of other children born with the same abnormality who'd had successful corrective surgery. He reassured my parents that I would be just fine and told them that other than the facial deformity, I was a perfectly healthy seven-and-a-half-pound boy. After having endured the loss of their stillborn daughter, Mom and Dad couldn't have been happier. I was alive and my problem could be fixed. That was all that mattered. And when Dr. Harris promised to personally do all of my surgeries at no cost to the family, they were even more relieved.

It would be several days before Mom and Dad could hold me. Even then they couldn't do it for long. I had tubes everywhere, so there wasn't a lot of physical contact. Unlike the Ship of Theseus, the Ship of Kevin was going to need a few planks replaced right away.

Mom had to feed me from an eyedropper because I couldn't breast feed or eat any other way. There was no Google to tell parents how much to feed their babies, so Mom continued to feed me from the eyedropper for a year. At my six-month checkup I weighed around ten pounds. The pediatrician told Mom that I was extremely underweight and asked her how much she'd been feeding me.

"This much," my mother said, indicating a few ounces on the dropper.

"Are you kidding me?" replied the horrified pediatrician. "Maybe that was enough when he was two months old, but by now he should be getting five times that much!"

"Oh, I had no idea!" Mom said. "He seems fine to me. He never cries and always seems happy, so I thought I was doing the right thing . . ."

That's my mother. Lovably oblivious. I'm happy to report that I inherited her "if it ain't broke, don't fix it" approach to life. Mom freely admits how life was back in the late '70s when I was born. Everyone smoked, no one wore seatbelts, and having a few glasses of wine now and then while pregnant wasn't a social death sentence. She says both of her boys were born "just fine" . . . lovably oblivious to the fact that my severe birth defect may have been caused by some of those very conditions. There still is no conclusive research that explains why cleft palates occur, and ultimately Mom is not wrong: we are just fine.

My maternal grandmother, on the other hand, was convinced I was going to have "a hard time becoming a man" because of the lack of physical contact I received as a young child. While my brother and cousins were being tossed in the air and wrestled with by my dad and uncles, I had to be treated with kid gloves physically. One day when I was a preschooler, as my grandmother watched my mother chop Fig Newtons into tiny pieces so I could eat them, she shook her head and said, "I'm afraid Kevin's going to grow up 'a little light in the loafers,' if you know what I mean." Her generation, the generation who lived through the Great Depression, wasn't used to pampering kids the way I had to be pampered. She loved me like crazy though, as did the rest of my tight-knit Irish-Italian family.

My mother was a secretary at the United Nations when I was young. She grew up in Queens, where her father was a police officer and her mother was a homemaker. My grandparents lived in the same house for fifty years, and that house was our extended family's social center. We went there often. I loved my uncles: Mom's older brother, Eddie (who, like his dad, was also a cop in New York City), and her younger brother, Tom. My grandparents saved up enough money to send only one of their kids to college, and Tom was The Chosen One. He headed off to university bearing the burden of knowing that his parents had put all their money on him, and he didn't disappoint. He became a successful banker with homes in New York and Florida. My uncles and their families were a lot of fun to be around when I was a kid. They still are.

And then there was my father. We don't know much about his side of the family, unfortunately. Dad's father died of a heart attack at the age of forty, so I never met him. Dad had one sibling, a brother who lived in Chicago with his wife and three kids. This brother died of a heart attack in his mid-thirties after being mugged during a business trip to New York City. We never really got to know his kids, our cousins. I did know and had a good relationship with my paternal grandmother though, who lived into her nineties.

Dad had grown up in Brooklyn and was the typical New York, East Coast dad of that era. Never said "I love you." Rarely hugged us. After Daniel and I were over the age of ten or so, he stopped showing us any real outward affection. He shook our hands instead. Dad was the guy who went off to his job at the New York Stock Exchange every weekday (he had a five-hour round trip commute) and came home to play catch and serve as Disciplinarian in Chief on nights and weekends. Despite his emotional detachment, he was a good and supportive dad. He loved us the best way he knew how.

Lastly, there's my brother, Daniel. He and I never really got along growing up. I thought he was a born kiss ass. Daniel was the classic A-student/class president/popular guy . . . and for most of my childhood I was the opposite of that. Still, we loved each other and looked out for each other. We would become much closer as we got older.

This was my tribe, my support team, my pit crew . . . and man, was I going to need them. Growing up with my kind of physical gifts, challenges, intellect, and attitude wasn't going to be easy.

A WORK IN PROGRESS

When I was very young I had some procedures done that allowed me to breathe a little easier, but the rest of the surgeries would play out over the course of my childhood into young adulthood. They couldn't do reconstructive surgeries on me too early because my growth would only undo what they'd just fixed. Simply put, getting a new-and-improved face was going to be a lengthy process. The first surgery I remember is when they put a bone in my nose to create two nostrils. I was probably seven or eight. As promised, Dr. Harris did the surgery with my parents paying nothing out-of-pocket. The man was a saint. When I was bitten by a dog at age four, he even came to the emergency room and stitched up my face for free. Over the years he and my parents became good friends. He was always there when we needed him.

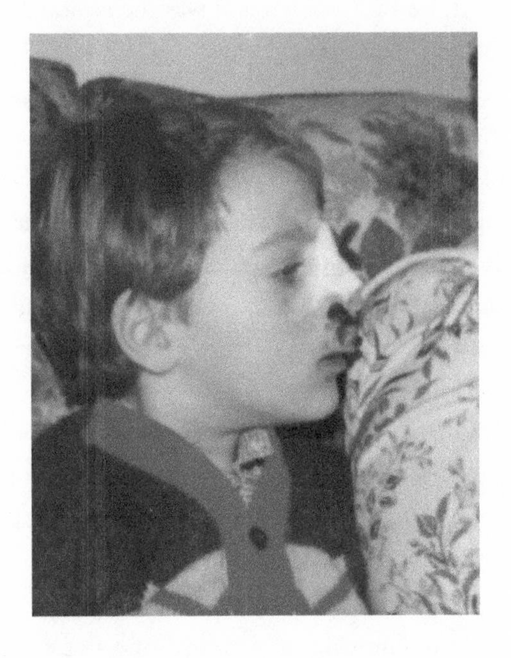

Because the inside of my mouth was a constantly changing canvas with holes leading to my nose and foreign objects to support the roof of my mouth, learning to talk efficiently was going to take work . . . a lot of work. My speech therapy started in early childhood and continued for decades. After every surgery I'd have to learn to talk all over again because the inside of my mouth had been altered. Consequently, I was super quiet when I was little (that would change drastically as I got older . . . more on that later). My lack of speech made it hard for my family to know what was going on in my mind. I found ways to let them know, though. My mom tells the story of one day when I was around eighteen months old.

She had run my bath, put me into the tub, and told me to sit down. I wouldn't sit down. She told me to sit down again. I wouldn't sit down. Again she told me to sit down and warned me that this time she meant it. I wouldn't sit down. She reached over and smacked my butt harder than she wanted to . . . so hard it left a welt. I didn't say a word. I didn't cry. I didn't even flinch. I just stared at her like a creepy horror movie baby. Mom says she was never more scared of a toddler in her life. When I saw her move her hand to pick up the washcloth, I sat down nice and slow, on my own damn terms. I guess to a degree I was born tough and stubborn.

Mom also tells the story of taking my brother and me for IQ testing at this preschool we were going to on Long Island. Mom sat in a waiting area while the teacher took us into another room to administer the tests. Afterward she brought us out to Mom with this amazed look on her face.

"Mrs. Cassidy, do you realize how smart your son is?" she asked.

"Oh yes! Daniel is very intelligent," Mom replied.

"No, I'm talking about Kevin! He has an extraordinarily high IQ, borderline genius. He will be able to learn without ever opening a book."

Mom had a hard time believing my IQ was higher than Daniel's. That's because Daniel was vocal and I was not, largely because I couldn't be. As Mom puts it, "Daniel was born wanting to shine!" When Daniel learned to tell time, everyone knew it because he told them. Me? Not so much. One day when I was around nine years old, someone in the room asked what time it was and I replied, "It's five o'clock."

"What?" Mom said, looking all surprised. "How do you know that?"

"There's a clock right there," I said, nodding toward the clock.

"But when did you learn to tell time?"

"I don't know . . . a couple years ago?"

"We never knew what you knew," Mom told me recently, "because you didn't tell us."

I didn't tell anybody what I knew. I was just kind of quiet . . . quietly confident, from a very young age. And like I said before, Mom was lovably oblivious.

Looking back on the origin of my self-confidence, I believe it sprang from two sources. First, I was born with it to some extent. "Confident" was part of my Who from day one. Second, the fact that my parents didn't pigeonhole me as a sad little deformed kid in my early years helped my innate confidence take root and grow stronger. My mom being lovably oblivious, my dad practicing tough love, and the culture and environment they themselves grew up in made this parenting style the obvious choice for them. I honestly don't think it was even a conscious one. Anything but this approach would have been unnatural for them.

I remember being prepped for a surgery when I was 7 or 8 years old and having serious opinions about not going through with it. I was freaked out and had a strong, nagging feeling in the pit of my soul that something was going to go wrong in the operating room. I threw an epic fit as I was being rolled toward the operating room door. Dr. Harris and my parents calmly agreed to hold off the surgery. All the prep work, scheduling logistics, time and effort my parents and Dr. Harris spent to get me to that door was now wasted. All of the adults seemed stoic about it though. My parents felt that it was only really hurting me and prolonging my journey of having a fully functioning face. If my dad were alive today, I imagine he would say something like, "If he wants to take the long hard road we'll watch him suffer through it until he changes his mind." He didn't view me as a vulnerable, sick child, he saw me as a strong-willed one capable of making it through the hard times knowing I'd be better off because of it.

Having the freedom to fail is a very precious gift. I was presented this gift many, many times while growing up in my household and am now stronger and more capable because of it. I'm sure it was mentally, and at times physically, taxing on my parents but they stayed the course and did what parents are supposed to do. Prepare their kids to be independent, strong, positive members of society. All parents, but especially parents of children with disabilities, have an important choice to make: dwell on their child's limitations and protect them from life, or give them the freedom to fail and to find their strength in order to build their confidence. My parents were shaping my Who since birth in this way. They were allowing me to find and replace my own internal planks while the doctors were busy replacing the external ones . . . when I'd let them.

A CHANGE OF SCENERY

In 1987, when I was ten years old and Daniel was twelve, our parents sat us down and told us that we were going to be moving. Not just across town but across several states, to Charlotte, North Carolina. It was exciting and sad at the same time. I remember getting my school yearbook signed on the last day of class and everyone writing, "Have fun in SC!" We were moving to North Carolina, but everybody wrote SC for some reason. I'm not sure why I remember that, yet I can't recall the name of even one of my teachers in New York. In my ten-year-old mind, it felt like we were going away to summer camp, not going away forever. Besides, there was something about North Carolina that Daniel and I were extremely excited about: our beloved Uncle Eddie and his family were there.

Sometime during the 1970s, Uncle Eddie was shot while working his beat in Harlem. He recovered and went back to the force for a while, but eventually he decided that he'd had enough of policing and Big Apple politics. He cashed in his retirement, loaded up his wife and four kids, and got out of New York City. They settled in Greensboro, North Carolina, where Eddie bought a Carvel ice cream store. Every year we'd take a road trip down there and have a great time with Uncle Eddie and our cousins. And every year Uncle Eddie would try to talk my parents into moving south. He recommended nearby Charlotte as a booming small city with good schools, where it would be easy for my parents to find work close to home. My mom and my dad—who did not enjoy his five-hour daily commute to work—finally agreed that North Carolina was the place for us.

Up to that point I hadn't experienced any bullying or teasing from my classmates that I remember. Two reasons for that, I assume: first, very small kids don't usually engage in bullying, and second, my classmates had known me since the beginning. They were used to the way I looked, the way I spoke. They'd watched me make progress from preschool through the fourth grade. Maybe they even felt a little bit of ownership in my progress.

But the kids in Charlotte? They'd never seen anything like me before, and they would become determined to make sure I knew that. They would remind me of it every chance they got. In no uncertain terms.

Every single day.

For years.

2

THE "MOVE OVA" KID

It's time you realized that you have something in you more powerful and miraculous than the things that affect you and make you dance like a puppet.

—MARCUS AURELIUS

IT'S NOT EASY BEING THE NEW KID IN SCHOOL, but it was really not easy being the new kid with a major speech impediment and a deformed face. I would find out just how "not easy" it was on my very first day, when the school bus arrived to pick me up. I boarded to find that all the seats were already taken. Some kids were having to sit three to a seat. I walked up and down the aisle a few times but nobody made room for me. Eventually my New York attitude kicked in.

"Hey, move ova," I said to one boy, my stiff Long Island accent instantly exposing the fact that I wasn't from around these parts.

"What'd you say?" he replied.

"I said move ova, I gotta siddown."

"'Move ova'? What the hell does that mean?" he laughed, elbowing the kid beside him. "Move ova! Move ova!"

It wasn't long until practically everyone on the bus was chanting, "Move ova! Move ova!"

Welcome to Dixie, Yankee boy . . .

Everything went downhill from there. It was as if these people spoke a different language. I quickly learned that if you wanted someone to make room for you, you were supposed to ask them to "scoot over," not "move ova." Even the teachers had a funny way of asking for what they wanted. I remember the first time I heard a teacher tell the class to "put your books up." I just sat there looking up, very confused. She called me out by name, demanding that I put my books up. I again looked up for someplace to put my books. She thought I was being disrespectful, but honestly, I had no idea what she meant. I later learned that in the South, to put something "up" means to put it away. I had a similar bewildering experience the first time a teacher asked me to "cut off the lights" so we could watch a film. I literally looked for scissors to cut the lights with, thinking that maybe these people didn't have the same kind of electricity we had in New York.

Not only did I have to adjust to Southern semantics, I also had to adjust to frequent bullying. Looking back, I can't say that there was any single incident that stood out as worse than the others. Instead it was just this constant mockery, this relentless tormenting. When kids hit those grades of five through seven, they naturally get more aggressive. Bullying and being picked on increases greatly. It could have (and probably would have) happened to me in New York as well. Not to the same extent, perhaps, but I doubt I would have gone my whole life in New York without getting some of the same treatment I received in North Carolina.

I never thought it was that terrible when I was going through it, though. In fact, to this day my mother will tell you she had no idea I was being bullied so much. I never brought it home with me and certainly never asked my parents to intervene on my behalf. Although I didn't enjoy being bullied, I also didn't internalize it to the point that it became my Who. In my view it was just another plank on the Ship of Kevin . . . a plank I could toss overboard when I didn't want to think about it anymore. To me, being picked on was just another thing to deal with, and every ten-year-old has a list of things they're dealing with. For some reason I never thought I had it worse than anyone else. The challenges I was facing were undoubtedly more obvious and easy targets, but no more daunting than those of the kid from a broken home, or the one with an abusive parent, or the one with a learning disability he's trying to hide. In a way it was beneficial that I *couldn't* hide what I was dealing with. I was forced to tackle it head on.

SPEAKING OF TACKLING . . .

Offsetting the challenges of my facial deformity was my athletic talent. I loved sports from a young age. I loved it because I was good at it and because it was a positive outlet for me. On the field, everyone treats you how you should be treated based on your ability, the only objective thing in life. There aren't a bunch of different variables there. It doesn't matter what you look like or sound like. If you're good, you're going to play. Luckily for me, I was exceptionally good. My parents supported me in all my athletic endeavors and made it possible for me to try lots of different things (something I recommend that all parents do, not just in athletics but in the arts and sciences, too). I received a major jolt of confidence from my involvement in sports, shoring up my self-assurance even more.

I'm sure this was very hard for my parents who only a few years before were still cutting up my food for me. All the fears my grandmother had of me not growing up to be tough because I wasn't held enough or roughhoused with as a small child were quickly culled. As soon as my feet were under me, I was full speed and no fear. While racing BMX in NY my grandmother couldn't bear to watch me whip around the track with reckless abandon. Maybe I was making up for all the missed roughhousing as a child or maybe I was just programed this way. Either way, to my parents' chagrin at times, I was wild, free, and full speed ahead when it came to anything physical like sports. That did not pair well with continuous facial surgeries, though. Kids don't think about that. They don't have the ability to look into the future further than tomorrow. Parents do. My parents threw their hands in the air and said, "I guess he'll learn the hard way," like they did when they moved that surgery, many times during my life.

Although I was well accepted on my sports teams, I continued to have a rough time at school. Talking was hard for me since I had only a couple of awkward teeth in the front and not much of an upper lip (it was smooshed down flat). Every time I spoke, the other kids would mimic me. By fifth grade I was talking a lot, trying to be the class clown in an attempt to win them over. I was very quick-witted, funny, and got a lot of laughs. Because of the way my mouth and nose were constructed, I could put sunflower seeds in my mouth and spit the shells out my nose. That was a good party trick that made the kids laugh, and in a way, I learned to embrace my deformity. Finally, I had some positive reinforcement. The laughter was a temporary reprieve from the mockery, and I needed that.

I had speech therapy a few times a week where I had to do drills to try to talk less nasally, to slow my speech, to articulate better. I would be called out of my classroom for these sessions by a voice over a loudspeaker:

"Kevin Cassidy, come to the office for speech therapy. Kevin Cassidy . . ."

I'd gather my stuff and head for the door to a chorus of giggles and wisecracks. It was like a walk of shame I had to endure twice a week for ten years.

My stomach dropped a little every time someone made fun of the way I talked, but only for a few minutes. Oddly enough, the way I heard my speech was different than how everyone else heard it. I couldn't hear the impediment and I often forgot I had one. The constant ridiculing served as my reminder.

The first time the speech therapist recorded me and I heard my own voice from a different perspective, the wind was knocked out of me. I was supremely embarrassed. I thought to myself, "If I heard myself sounding like that, I would never talk!" Fortunately for me I didn't hear myself like that. Unfortunately for everyone else that meant I was going to talk a lot even despite all the teasing.

Like the fictional football-coach-turned-soccer-coach Ted Lasso says, "be a goldfish." Goldfish only have ten-second memories. When you make a mistake in a fast-moving game, you can't dwell on it in the moment, you have to move past it quickly. You can revisit it later and learn from it, but in the moment it's best to be a goldfish. When it came to my speech impediment and physical appearance, I was a goldfish. I was able to compartmentalize a lot of things, move them to the back of the brain in the moment, and recall them later when I had time and the ability to focus on them. This had pros and cons. It allowed me the freedom and confidence to navigate through my day-to-day life, but it also set me up for more mockery and bullying, which, at the end of the day, enabled me to hone and perfect being a goldfish.

I think this ability was a byproduct of a fast-moving and constantly changing life. It is a skill I've utilized countless times. Without it, for me, the goal of humble confidence and a Who-driven life would be impossible. I was recorded a lot at speech therapy and every time I heard myself on tape I cringed at how I sounded, and, every time, within an hour I'd completely forget about it and start yapping again . . . until someone would remind me that I sounded like I had a mouthful of marbles or until my next speech session, and the pattern would repeat.

FAMILY UPHEAVAL

I wasn't the only one who had a hard time adjusting to life in North Carolina. My dad had difficulty finding a job and was unemployed for an extended period. Mom went to work as a secretary again, becoming our family's sole breadwinner. When Dad finally did get a job, it was as a janitor and bus driver at what would eventually be my high school.

For seventh grade I was bused across town to a horrible junior high. Violence was the general vibe at this school. You'd accidently bump into a kid in the hallway and he'd punch you in the face. I remember a big gang fight my first year there. No shooting, but knives, chains, and other weapons were involved. I was bullied and beat up often at this school. It wasn't only because of my birth defect and speech impediment, although that certainly continued to be a trigger. Once I started playing sports and had established myself as a competitive athlete, I had an even bigger bullseye on my back.

I had one particularly unpleasant teacher who was very aggressive toward me. On the first day she seemed to hold a grudge against me despite the fact that I'd just met her. I couldn't do anything right. She once contacted my parents and accused me of doing something terrible (I don't remember what it was because I didn't do it). I told my parents the teacher was lying.

"Your teacher would *never* lie," my mom said. "And since she's not lying, *you* must be lying."

My parents believed that every teacher was right even when the evidence showed the contrary. Probably another characteristic embedded in them from the way they grew up in New York. All the times they threw their hands in the air while letting me find out the hard way had evolved into a feeling of indifference toward me. Looking back at it now, it seems to be a natural mental progression. How long can one let a child walk his own path before you detach yourself from that child a little for your own sanity? As a result of this, my mother and father never gave me the benefit of the doubt in any situation where it was my word against that of an authority figure. This was a very hard pill for me to swallow. I couldn't comprehend that a person would take sides based on the people involved as opposed to the facts involved. Just because I was a child, I was wrong. That's something I do not agree with to this day. However, at the end of the day, as a parent you have to make a call. My parents' default call was to side against me and make me feel like my voice didn't matter. It was the opposite of what's happening in society now, where so many parents believe their child can do no wrong. They blindly side with the child and make the other side feel as if their voice holds no weight. There is a middle ground here . . . you can discipline the child while ensuring their voice is heard, and you can vindicate the child while ensuring the other voice is being heard as well.

I think about this a lot now that I'm a father. In my view it is critical that parents walk this line carefully and don't blindly adhere to the notion that either the teacher or the child is always right. We should take the time to view each situation on its own merits and take into account the people and unique circumstances involved. Children need to feel like their opinions matter, but they also need to know that most adults (not all adults, and certainly not just because they are adults) have their best interest in mind. It's about cultivating mutual respect from an early age and not giving it freely to anyone who hasn't earned it, no matter how late in life they may be. But I digress . . .

Because of my disappointment with my family's lack of faith in me and my classmates' constant harassment, I became intolerant of disrespect. I fought anyone who challenged me. I ignored the first, second, and sometimes even the third comment about my teeth, my face, or my speech but once I acknowledged it, fists immediately started to fly. Experience taught me that if I opened my mouth first to try to diffuse the situation, my speech impediment would make them laugh louder and give them more energy, so I learned quickly to either walk away or fight. I did an equal amount of both. Over time, I could see the bullies weighing their options, wondering if it was worth it to make fun of me. I and everyone around me were figuring out where the line was drawn . . . a stray comment was fine and I often laughed along with it if it was funny, but the in-your-face disrespectful comment was answered with a fist. I was strong and athletic and didn't mind standing my ground when I felt it necessary.

That, the constant mockery, and the declining faith in my household moved my "give-a-shit meter" to empty. If you don't give a shit, you don't think ahead. Because of that I never thought about consequences. There was no tomorrow in my adolescent mind and I committed to the present. If the decision I made in that present led me to the hospital or to be expelled, I'd deal with those issues in their present. They never occurred to me in the moment and because of that I was able to fully commit—physically and emotionally—to whatever happened to be in front of me. Eventually I was able to hone this skill and use it in a myriad of beneficial ways, but at this point in my life it served more as a defense mechanism.

When the momma bear sees her cubs in danger she no longer thinks about preparing for hibernation; she is solely focused on one task: destroy whatever is threatening her babies. If that takes her down the river and away from her cave, so be it. This mentality no doubt enables the bear to protect her young to the best of her ability and is an intricate part of her DNA and evolutional makeup. It may also be the reason they all freeze to death or starve in the coming winter. The ability to not look back or ahead had its pros and cons. As I worked through them, without knowing it, I was building the foundation of my Who. It is beneficial to be able to focus on the task at hand with no distractions of previous paths or future consequences, but this ability is a double-edged sword. Many planks on the Ship of Kevin were damaged beyond repair and had to be replaced during my adolescence because I was busy protecting my cubs and found myself too far down river.

In defense of my young classmates and teammates who were bullying me, their treatment was actually pretty normal. No matter where we find ourselves, if we are different from the others around us, we will be treated as The Other. Groups of people are territorial and don't take kindly to threats from the outside. Sooner or later, if you live your life freely, you will find yourself as an outsider. You can choose to learn from this experience and use it to better understand the world around you or run back to your comfort zone. Since I didn't have a comfort zone I was forced to learn from these experiences. That knowledge has helped fuel my success in life in ways that I couldn't imagine back then. For some reason I understood this social phenomenon early on and tried not to take things too personally. Most of the time I succeeded, but sometimes I didn't. Not taking things too personally is a lot easier said than done. I was forced to start learning the skills necessary to achieve this very early in life and in a way was blessed that I never knew any different. I was constantly forced to compartmentalize things emotionally, socially, and physically, since before I could remember.

In junior high most kids were just starting to work this out for themselves, but I had years of experience and was much further down the path of discovery than they were. When a friend would take a jab at my speech in front of a girl, it annoyed me but I didn't erase the friendship because of it. Being able to know who to forgive and who to fight seemed very natural to me. I guess I was lucky to be able to see multiple sides of people at a young age. I was able to decipher their true character quickly and accurately, and always gave the benefit of the doubt when I could. I valued the good over the bad, but if a situation escalated and led to a fight, I didn't let that moment define their Who and would be able to forgive them (internally at least) fairly quickly. I remember actively trying to turn this off so I could hate people and not stay in an endless loop of being friends, being annoyed, fighting because they crossed the line, and back to being friends again but I was never able to. I was yearning for this benefit of the doubt personally as well, for my good to outweigh my bad, and as a result I was unable to project anything but this onto others.

As junior high went on and my battles both internally and externally continued, my brother Daniel somehow existed on the outskirts of all this drama. He was able to navigate that world more seamlessly than I was. He found a good group of friends and for the most part was able to get by without mingling with the roughnecks too much. Those two worlds were bound to collide every now and then, though, and I remember one specific instance when they did. Word was going around school that, for whatever reason, a couple of guys I knew from the football team were going to beat up my brother. I was able to get there in time and tried to diffuse the situation, but ultimately, I ended up getting in a fight with those guys myself while Daniel ran off. The fight got broken up pretty quickly and I figured that was the end of it. But at dinner that night—we always had dinner as a family—my brother told our parents that I got in a fight at school.

"I got in a fight because of you!" I replied. "*I was protecting you!*"

Didn't matter. I was the one who got in trouble. Just another example of nobody in my household giving me the benefit of the doubt, even when I did something honorable. This was becoming the norm at home, and for a moment I let it break my heart. I was able to compartmentalize the experiences I had with my peers because those experiences were so varied and there was good to take with the bad, but more and more throughout junior high the experience in my home was consistently soul sucking for me. I never hated them but I developed a deep sense of apathy for my immediate family during this time in my life. The deep-seeded forgiveness and understanding I was cultivating with my peers was eventually able to be transferred to my family, though. A little too late, I'm afraid, and only because of a tragedy, as you'll learn about later, but luckily my internal seeds of forgiveness are hard to kill.

My parents were still very outwardly supportive of me, though. They took me to all my practices and games, cheered for me in the stands, and became friends with my teammates' parents. But the minute we walked through the door of our house, mutual apathy filled the air. It wasn't fake. They genuinely were proud of the son they had on the field. Something about the forced increased space between us made it easy for them and me to coexist in a positive way. When that space was removed, indifference set in. Neither of us knew how to get through to the other, and deep down I'm sure that broke my parents' hearts as it did mine.

I still wanted to be the happy, fun, energic kid that it was my nature to be, but that possibility only existed outside of my house. I closed myself off from my family and opened myself up to anyone else who would extend that benefit of the doubt I longed for. Only problem was, I couldn't always find many people who were willing to give me that courtesy.

The bullying was in full swing by then, and much of it still centered on my appearance and speech. Until the seventh grade, my mouth was essentially roofless and toothless except for the two front teeth, earning me the unfortunate nickname of Rat Boy. Rat Boy stuck with me all through junior high, and although I never considered it a term of endearment, I learned to answer to it.

3

FROM RAT BOY TO TEAM CAPTAIN

If you know the enemy and know yourself, you need not fear the result of a hundred battles. If you know yourself but not the enemy, for every victory gained you will suffer a defeat. If you know neither the enemy nor yourself, you will succumb in every battle.

—SUN TZU, *THE ART OF WAR*

IN THE SEVENTH GRADE I HAD A MAJOR SURGERY: Dr. Harris and his team took bone out of my hip and used it to construct a roof for my mouth. When I returned to school, I still had a bunch of gauze and other medical contraptions in my mouth and had to walk on crutches for weeks. Of course, my speech impediment was even worse than before because I was learning to use a brand-new mouth. That didn't prevent me from talking, though. I continued trying to make my classmates laugh with my quick and witty commentary.

Several days after I got back to school following the surgery, I was called to my homeroom teacher's office. She sat me down and asked me if I smelled what everyone else was smelling. I'd never had a good sense of smell, but I certainly didn't have one now, not with all that stuff in my mouth. I told her I had no idea what she was talking about.

"Well, ever since you had your surgery there's been a terrible odor coming from your mouth," she said. "I can smell it clear over here. The other kids can smell it, too. It's really bad, Kevin. Your parents should talk to your doctor and find out what's going on."

Jesus Christ! Now—on top of everything else—I stink? And everyone in the world knows it but me?

I was sent home from school that day, this weird smelly kid who everyone was repelled by. Mom called the doctor and learned that there was nothing to be done: the odor was a natural side effect of the surgery. I'd just have to live with it until it went away. At that point I became extremely self-conscious about talking, because I knew that when I opened my mouth the smell was bad . . . so bad it caused people to want to move away from me. Bad enough that my goldfish-short-term memory was no match for it, and I didn't need to be reminded of it. It forced me to shut up a little bit and take in my surroundings. Although my brain continued to think up a million funny things to say, I bit my tongue and kept my mouth closed. This would turn out to be one of the best things that ever happened to me.

MY SOCIAL EXPERIMENT

There's a funny thing that happens when you take a vow of silence and essentially cloister yourself: suddenly you have time to observe your world and everyone in it. Through that observation—forced observation, in my case—I began to understand the finer points of social interaction.

Naturally, my observations started out with girls I liked. As I watched them interact with others (and interact with me on a limited basis now that I was keeping my mouth shut most of the time) I was able to see how most exchanges started off fine but deteriorated the longer they lasted. In my case, I'd be funny and make a girl laugh, but I didn't know when to stop. Eventually I'd annoy her, and she'd walk away. In this situation I was forced to look at how that interaction ended and digest her feelings about it. With time I got better at analyzing girls' body language and facial expressions so that I could detect the exact moment that I was beginning to go too far, and I could apply the brakes. I'd back off and make a conscious effort to be a little distant to them (yet still nice) for the rest of the week until I got back in their good graces. It worked every time.

My success inspired me to apply the same experiment to my interactions with my other classmates, teachers, coaches, and teammates. I found that it worked with everybody. By shutting up and paying attention, I started to figure out who was insecure, who was shy, who was stuck up or ultra-sensitive. Who could take a joke, who was trustworthy, who was lonely, and who was a natural born jerk. I learned to make these assessments accurately and quickly. I watched not just how people reacted to me but to others, making mental notes of what set them off, when, and by whom. I paid particular attention to which guys the girls liked and committed to memory the things they were doing right. During this forced vow of silence, I was able to build upon, accelerate, and consciously identify the things I was compartmentalizing years before. I found out that I had subconsciously already done a lot of the leg work to internalize these things, but I was now learning how to put that into real-world practice. It was a similar epiphany to the one that married The Ship of Theseus Paradox to the Who vs. What philosophy.

The most valuable thing I learned from my experiment was how to identify my role in each individual relationship I had. I learned to accept my relationships for what they were. For example, if I liked a girl but read her well enough to know that I didn't have a chance with her romantically,

I would settle for being a friend to her instead of pursuing her. Or if I discerned through observation that someone was an ass, I quit caring what they thought of me and limited my interaction with them. I quit trying to win them over.

I enjoyed having this new information, this new understanding of my world. I felt in control . . . a feeling I'd lacked in so many aspects of my life up to then. I became even more quiet, and consequently became a better student as well. I grew emotionally and socially, and—most importantly—learned to channel my anger. By ninth grade I had figured out almost everyone in my social orbit and had a very optimistic view of my future. This was accomplished in part by being the momma bear protecting her cubs. School, sports, and friends were the cubs that I successfully protected. My family, however, was the cave I found myself too far downstream to reach.

By the time I got to high school I was dialed in on a social level that most people weren't. The bullying decreased significantly, and though the stray comments were always around, the big fights stopped happening for the most part. I still had a chip on my shoulder for anyone who disrespected me, though. I thought it was my job to check people's egos and knock them down a peg for the greater good (especially now that, in my mind, I knew who deserved it the most). But I became friends with a lot of the people who were beating me up the years before. I never held a grudge because through my social interactions I saw how the people around me were changing, maturing, and dealing with their own issues. The benefit of the doubt that I gave people in the past bore a lot of fruit in this future. For the most part, everyone I've ever met has some good in them—even if they were beating me up a few years before.

I think this ability to observe and analyze the people around us is one of the most powerful skills we can learn. It makes life so much easier, so much more meaningful and interesting. Try it for yourself. You'll see. And if you are an adult with young people in your life, do them a huge favor and encourage them to develop their social observation and analysis skills, too. You can be sure I'll be teaching this stuff to my daughters.

I'll also be teaching them to think of their social roles as planks on their personal Ships of Theseus. Just because you've been playing a certain role so far (a What) doesn't mean you have to keep doing it, especially if it's making your life harder than it has to be. If a What is causing you pain, you owe it to yourself to remove that plank. You can then patch the hole with a stronger, healthier plank; one that buoys you rather than sinks you. One that sustains you rather than drains you. Rebuilding your ship so you can keep on sailing: that's what personal growth is all about.

REBUILD YOUR SHIP AND KEEP ON SAILING.

NEW SCHOOL, NEW ROLE

By the time I got to high school, everything had changed for me. Thanks to lots of surgeries, dental work, and speech therapy, I finally looked fairly normal and talked well enough. I wore a retainer with a bunch of false teeth attached to it, but that was no big deal. Ha! Imagine that . . . going through all of high school having to wear a retainer 100% of the time and being excited about it. Man, I was "lovably oblivious" just like my mother. Thank God!

The good news was that more than half the students at this school had never met me before, so any preconceived notions about me being an ugly Rat Boy were almost non-existent. And with the social knowledge I'd accumulated during the last two years of junior high, I had confidence that I could carve out my role however I wanted it to be. Like most teenage boys I wanted to be accepted, not tormented, and possibly even popular. It wasn't long before I was, for the first time in my life. It happened naturally and I was soon friends with girls and boys at every level of our school's social order.

Being a well-liked athlete who was great with everyone socially was awesome, except I still had a mouth full of fake teeth and zero experience on a romantic level. This made for some awkward moments. My confidence was unshakable but my reluctance to make a move with a girl kept my ego in check. That turned out to be a great equalizer. I knew when a girl liked me but I played the cool standoffish jock so as not to expose myself as the guy who still hadn't kissed a girl . . . even as a senior on the Homecoming King ballot. That finally came to an end when a girl I'd gone out with a few times got me cornered and planted one on me. Retainer full of fake teeth and all, we made out, very awkwardly (for me at least). Like a professional poker player, she never flinched. Going all in with nothing, she was a rock. We made out a few more times over the next several weeks but I never got in the groove. I couldn't get past how she must feel (and honestly *what* she must feel) with her tongue in my retainer-filled mouth.

That retainer! When I played football I'd have to take it out so I could wear my mouth guard and my teeth would come out along with it. My teammates would say, "Oh, I forgot you had no teeth!" I had fun with it, but only as long as there were no girls around.

Sports continued to play a huge role in my life during high school. I was the only sophomore to make the varsity football team. I was a linebacker, safety, and wide receiver. Football was easy for me because I had all the natural abilities as well as the intangibles it takes to play the sport well: speed, vision, toughness, and controlled aggression. I didn't take well to the football mentality though, and I wasn't crazy about our coach. One particular game during my senior year against our much-better city rivals, I had a touchdown, an interception, and had made twelve tackles in the first half, and we were winning 6–0. The coach berated me at halftime in the locker room, telling me to stop smiling; that I was supposed to be "tough" and "angry" because "this is football!" I didn't have to be angry to be tough. Tough was my default. I got hurt in the third quarter of that game and we lost 52–6. I didn't understand why the coach had to take away the fun and comradery in exchange for toughness, as if those things can't coexist. There are football coaches who are more player-friendly and have fun with the sport, but I never got to play for one of them.

Sports were a great outlet, allowing me to release my pent-up aggression in a positive way, and I needed that. They were the foundational building blocks my character was built upon. Of course, I didn't know it at the time and like everything in my life I didn't feel too attached to them. Positive things, like making the team, and negative things, like being bullied, ultimately fell into the same bucket for me: the What bucket. The bucket that even as a sophomore in high school I didn't take too seriously. For me that bucket was never full, as if it had holes in the bottom. The more Whats I filled it with, the more drained out the bottom. It was never able to hold any weight in my life. I took sports like I took everything else: it was just something I did.

My tendency toward detachment as a defense mechanism was tested severely at the beginning of my junior year. As I said before, I was one of the only sophomores to play on the varsity football team. I did very well and set myself up for dominating junior year. I played baseball all summer on an all-star travel team that I loved, and a few weeks before football practice started, I was playing in a baseball tournament and got injured. I pulled a hamstring running out a ground ball I hit and was gonna have to miss the first few weeks of football practice to recover. When I told my football coach this, he bluntly called me a pussy and told me to get out of his office. He hated that I wasted my football talent by playing baseball in the off-season instead of building my strength for the upcoming football season.

"You know what? Screw you!" I said. "You don't respect me—I won't play at all!"

Much to everyone's surprise, I kept my word. I didn't play football that year. The all-important junior year where the top colleges are looking for talent and where an athlete like myself could've separated from the pack and been on every big school's radar. The year before I was "so cool" and gained immense social points by being the youngest guy on the varsity team and I just threw it all away with no explanation. I'm sure everyone in my orbit was shocked. The only thing I regret about that decision is letting down my football teammates by not being on the field with them. My good friend and QB from that team is mad at me to this day as he swears if I would have played, he probably would've gotten a college scholarship. I watched the whole season from the stands with my friends. My parents and teammates couldn't believe I followed through on my threat but in all honesty, it didn't affect me negatively. I never took myself seriously enough or had anything reach me deeply enough that I couldn't leave it. I didn't have that sense of identity that made me declare "I Am a Football Player" or "I Am a Deformed Kid." I never got into any of those mentalities because I was forced to evolve so fast.

This fast-paced evolution is what poked the holes in my What bucket, not allowing it to fill up. At the same time, it reinforced and strengthened my Who bucket so it could hold more and more weight. As soon as one sports season ended, the next one started. As soon as I healed from one surgery, I had another. I didn't have time to only be a baseball player or a football player or a deformed kid. It was as if so many planks were being replaced on the Ship of Kevin so quickly I didn't have the time or energy to dwell over losing them. I just threw them overboard and moved on to the next one.

Playing sports served me well. It did more good for me than I realized at the time. It gave me a physical outlet, friendships, and a community. It gave me the benefit of the doubt I needed, built my confidence, kept me humble, and showed me where great leadership comes from. I can't imagine what my early years would have been like had I not been a competitive athlete. It would have been a lot tougher, that's for sure.

Even though things were going great for me at school socially, my parents continued to express their lack of faith in me. I'm sure they were as shocked as anyone about my decision to not play football my junior year. "Disappointed" is probably a better word, which is fair. But that uncomfortable air space around us when we occupied the same room was as strong as ever and because of it they never brought up or even talked to me about why I didn't play that year. We existed in two different planes of reality. The comfortable, detached one that existed when I was far enough away and the suffocating one that existed when we were under the same roof. Because of the lack of communication neither of us knew how or what the other was feeling. It came to a head one evening when I came home from school, though. They told me they needed to talk to me. They sat me down at the kitchen table. They were crying.

"What are you doing with your life, Kevin?" Dad said. "Are you on drugs?"

"Please tell us so we can help you!" Mom cried.

All the pent-up emotions they must have had poured out on the table that evening, and looking back, I'm sure they were scared as hell of where my life was going. But all I heard was that they thought I was the type of kid who was out stealing cars and doing drugs. That solidified the fact that they didn't know me at all. All of my friends were great students, most of whom were on sports teams and all of whom were on a clear path to college. I had no idea where any of this was coming from. How were they forming their opinion of me?!? I had no idea. I told them I was fine. I was not doing drugs or stealing cars or any of the other things they accused me of. I was busy with school and sports and had a great group of friends. Nothing I said convinced my parents that I was not the person that they had built up in their minds.

I remember one night in high school when I had made plans to go to a party of some sort. I of course lied to my parents about it because of their lack of faith in me. The phone rang and it was the parent of a good friend who was going to the party with me. This friend was honest with his parents, unlike me. His mom asked my mom if I was going to the party. Busted. I came clean and said "yes." To my mom's surprise, the woman on the other end of the phone kept talking and expressed that she wouldn't let her son go unless I was going. She was calling to make sure I was going to be there because she knew I looked out for everyone and felt better about allowing her son to go if I was going, too. This must have confused my mother tremendously. It's the first time I remember my two worlds colliding. I hoped it would get through to my parents that I was a good kid and open their eyes to how the rest of the world saw and treated me. Maybe it did a little. Maybe it planted a seed that needed time to grow, but in the moment, it was not enough to make a dent in the stale air of our house.

After a fun and extremely competitive junior year on the baseball field, I again played travel summer baseball but this time came out unscathed, which opened the door, physically at least, for me to play football my senior year. Everyone thought that bridge had burned, and I was committed to robbing the coach of my talent. But as you know by now, I'm not built like that. I missed football and wanted to get back on the field with my teammates. The coach had to let me try out again as it was an open tryout, and he had the option to cut me on principle if he wanted to—a reality I would deal with in time. All I had to do was show up. Showing up seemed to be a big deal for everyone except me. Life was simple to me. I wanted to play, and in order to do so, I show up at this field at this time. Period. Next. The coach didn't cut me. He didn't acknowledge me much, and he certainly didn't have a nice word to say to me all season, but I started every game and played extremely well. Up until I blew my shoulder out in the sixth game and my season ended, that is.

Emotionally, playing was the same as not playing for me. Neither was a part of my Who, so I was free to do what I wanted in the moment. I wasn't tied down by expectations, or other people's opinion. Humble confidence, a weak attachment to What, and a strong attachment to Who simplifies life in many ways and is very freeing.

Even though I didn't play football my junior year and got hurt six games into my senior year, I had a few scholarship offers on the table. I had a few on the table for baseball as well. I had done my freshman orientation and signed up for classes at one particular school, but a few weeks before school actually started, I got a call from a small D-II school about playing baseball for them. Lenoir-Rhyne University in Hickory, North Carolina, and a coach named Adams wanted me to come visit. I drove over—Hickory is only an hour from Charlotte—to meet the coach and check the place out. I liked what I saw. I appreciated the smaller school dynamic, and Coach Adams and I hit it off immediately. And of course, I liked baseball better than football. For those reasons I chose LRU.

Right after high school graduation, I had dental surgery to implant a complete bridge into my mouth, thereby eliminating the need for retainers and removable teeth. They cut into my gums and screwed a set of fake teeth into the bone. By the time I left for LRU, I looked better than ever, and I felt like a million bucks. I was ready to set sail.

4

THE MONTAGUES AND CAPULETS

If anyone tells you that a certain person speaks ill of you, do not make excuses about what is said of you but answer, "He was ignorant of my other faults, else he would have not mentioned these alone."

—EPICTETUS

I ARRIVED AS A FRESHMAN on the LRU campus knowing only two people: Coach Adams and a former high school teammate of mine who was starting his sophomore year and was on the LRU football team. Thanks to him, the first people I met and became friends with on campus were the football players. They were all very nice, stereotypically masculine and rough around the edges but right up my alley. They were quick to give me a hard time about being a baseball player and tried to get me to play football instead. I laughed off the good-natured ribbing, made some new friends, and was off to a good start socially during my first few weeks of college.

It was only after I met my baseball teammates that I realized there was an interesting dynamic at this school, namely that football and baseball players were like oil and water. They didn't mix. At least that seemed to be the expectation. While the football players were taunting me about being a baseball player, the baseball guys were razzing me about being friends with the football players. I was a baseball player on scholarship, so I guess my teammates felt some ownership of me. They were downright territorial about it. I thought it was silly. I ignored them and did my own thing.

Like many universities, LRU had a competitive intramural football league. The two best teams in that league were made up of baseball players on one and of red-shirted or ex-football players (active LRU football players weren't allowed to play intramurals) on the other. The baseball guys didn't ask me to play with them my freshman year because they didn't know how good I was, but my old high school buddy did. He convinced the football intramural team to invite me to play for them. I accepted the invitation because I wanted to play.

Inevitably the game schedule brought my team face-to-face against the baseball guys. When they saw me on the opposing sideline with the football team, the banter went something like this:

"Cass? What the hell are you doing?"

"I'm playing with the football guys."

"You can't play with the football guys, bro."

"Why not? They're friends of mine."

"But you're a baseball player! You can't play with the football guys!"

"The hell I can't! Did you ask me to be on your team?"

"No, but . . ."

"Well these guys did. So kiss my ass!"

Of course, the football guys watched all this with great amusement.

They decided to twist the knife a little bit and mess with the baseball guys, resulting in some after-the-whistle pushing and shoving as we played that game. Typical me, I didn't back down. I didn't care what anyone said. I was just being competitive and having fun. I didn't care too much about either side, to be honest. I stood my own ground. Both sides had a few assholes, but the large majority of guys would've been friends if this dynamic was removed, and I gravitated to these guys on both sides.

I've always found it funny when I see a person identify so strongly with a group that they can't identify with themselves anymore. Maybe "funny" isn't the right word because this tendency is a signal that there's a serious internal problem. Some people are so confused about Who they are as an individual that they can only focus on a What. This leads them to becoming tribal. This What becomes all-consuming and is the most important aspect of their being. They become closed-minded, one-dimensional, and lose their objectivity because of it. The sole focus on a What is similar to the momma bear focusing on protecting her cubs to the peril of all else. The problem in this scenario is that there are no cubs to protect. No ends to justify the means, and peril is all that is created. The only way out of this is in. Looking in. Searching your soul for something more than What you are. It's very hard to go through life propped up by What you are and change by looking internally. It takes a tremendous amount of humility and honesty. The longer you wait to look in the harder it becomes.

People—especially young people—aren't looking inward anymore. Their self-value is based on outside variables and if they don't like what they see, they take it out on other outside variables, which could very well be a key part in the mental health crisis we find ourselves in today. For some reason I didn't fall for that, and I hope you don't either. It's so much healthier to "Know Thyself," as the ancient Greeks used to say. Doing the internal work of getting to know your Who will hold you together when other people's ships start falling apart at the seams.

That's the way it worked out for me in my freshman year at LRU. The football guys respected my grit and attitude so much that they invited me to join their fraternity, Tau Kappa Epsilon, or TKE. They only gave out two or three invitations a year and no one ever turned them down because, among other things, they were known for having the coolest parties. They were also known as a football-only fraternity. No baseball types allowed. I was the first baseball player in recent memory to be offered an invitation to pledge. I was tempted to accept, but in the end, I turned them down. I felt that pledging a fraternity—any fraternity—might interfere with my focus on baseball. The TKE guys were not happy with that decision. Now I had both sides mad at me.

Although there was friction, I managed to remain friends with everyone. Because of my comfort with easing in and out of social roles based upon whatever dynamic was present in the moment, and my give-a-shit meter holding steady at zero, I was able to navigate pretty seamlessly through my freshman year despite the simmering tension. This could have gone sideways very easily, had I been the kind of person who gets wrapped up in a narrow identity (football player, baseball player, liberal, conservative, Yankee, Rebel, whatever). Instead, I decided to behave like Switzerland and maintain neutrality. Well, maybe not exactly like Switzerland . . . I did stay neutral but more like the way Sparta remained neutral. I didn't take sides, but I was willing to fight everyone to prove it.

I had a good baseball season my freshman year—so good that Coach Adams took it upon himself to arrange for me and two other teammates to play in an elite wooden bat league in Maryland over the summer, the Clark Griffith Collegiate League (CGL), with the University of Maryland being our home field. We were the only D-II players to make our team, the Maryland Bombers. We stayed in a frat house on campus with the other dozen or so out-of-towners. A few University of Maryland players were on the team as well, along with standout athletes from the University of Virginia, NC State, and other D-I baseball programs along the East Coast. My LRU teammates and I were given a fair shot at playing time and all three of us earned starting positions. Not only did I make the CGL All-Star team, but I also made a lot of good friends. It was one of the best summers of my life. Unfortunately, the good feelings were not meant to last.

K-CASS MEETS THE NEW COACH

Most eruptions start well below the surface. As temperatures rise and chemicals mix there comes a point of no return, and the only possible outcome is an epic explosion. This was as true about me in my sophomore year of college as it is of any volcanic eruption throughout history. To understand the magnitude of the explosion you first need to explore what was under the surface . . .

Over the summer, while my two teammates and I were still playing ball in Maryland, we received a call from Coach Adams delivering some sad news: his wife was seriously ill, and he was retiring to spend time with her. We were sad to see him go, but we understood that Coach had to do what he had to do. My buddies and I wished him well and returned to LRU a few weeks later eager to meet our new leader (I'll call him Coach Smith). He was relatively young—probably in his mid-thirties. He'd been an assistant coach on another team but this would be his first foray into head coaching. Smith had some insecurities, but I liked him immediately. Everyone got on well with him. He made an effort to be "one of the guys." He liked to laugh and have fun as long as we were getting things done and playing hard. He was a player's coach.

Because I was a strong returning player who'd competed in an elite league over the summer, I was an unofficial team leader. For that reason, and a few others I'll mention shortly, I feel like Coach Smith (inexperienced as he was) believed he needed to knock me down a peg to boost his status. He and I butted heads a little bit in practice, but not too much.

As the school year got underway, TKE offered me the chance to pledge their football fraternity again, and this time I took it. I didn't feel like tiptoeing around this stupid baseball-versus-football minefield anymore. I didn't think anyone should have to, frankly. I decided to put a stake in the ground and become a Freedom Fighter for LRU campus life. I was going to desegregate this fraternity and bring the athletes from both sports together once and for all. I had this fantasy of inviting all my fellow baseball players over to the TKE house for a party with my football frat brothers. We'd have a big Kumbaya moment around the keg and all the hostility would melt away in an instant. History would be made.

I wasn't alone in this pie-in-the-sky endeavor. Another baseball player, my roommate, Adam, pledged TKE with me. Whatever skills Adam lacked on the baseball field he made up for with an aggressive I-don't-give-a-shit mentality that made us great friends right away. A rough, tough New Yorker, he was the perfect partner to get this mission accomplished.

The TKE pledging process took a whole semester and consisted of all kinds of crazy pranks. One night the TKEs snuck into our room and kidnapped us and wouldn't let us go until we'd memorized a laundry list of ridiculous stuff. They made us do a bunch of embarrassing stunts around campus. I showed up for all of it but didn't take it too seriously, which was not appreciated by the frat and made things worse for me. I didn't care. It was all good-natured fun, but it took a lot of time and effort.

For that reason, Adam and I came to baseball practice with our butts dragging more than once. That didn't make Coach Smith very happy. Come to find out, he had strong opinions about fraternities. He thought, like many people did, that I was there to play baseball, not be in a frat. He viewed my joining TKE as a slap in the face to the baseball team and the loyalties that should exist there. I understand that mentality. Like a lot of coaches, he wanted everyone to be 100% focused on his world and put that above all else. Not my strong suit, and it caused some friction. The payoff was worth it, though. Adam and I made it into the TKEs, and to this day (to my knowledge) the baseball/football feud is no more.

After Christmas break the actual baseball season began. We won our first several games and I got off to a particularly hot start with my bat. One afternoon we were playing an away game and it seemed our growing momentum had run out and nothing was going right for us. We were losing the game, and nobody seemed to be handling it well. I struck out at some point in the middle innings and had a few words with the home plate umpire, to which Coach Smith chimed in from the third-base coaching box pretty much instructing me to shut my mouth and get back in the dugout. Which, of course, he was right to do. Only problem was, he didn't stop there. He kept yelling at me from across the diamond even after I'd reached our dugout on the first-base side. I couldn't understand what he was saying but I could tell he was pissed at me. Even after we took the field for defense, Coach kept his eyeball on me and yelled at me sporadically for the rest of the game. Finally—mercifully—the nine innings were over. We'd lost.

At the end of each game we always had a team meeting down the right field line. On this day as we gathered in the outfield with our heads hung low, Coach Smith chewed us out for our lack of focus and hustle. Then he turned to me.

"The people who are supposed to be leaders on this team didn't deliver today!" he shouted, looking straight at me but not saying my name. "These so-called leaders let this team down! They let themselves down!"

And so on and so forth. You get the idea. The longer and louder Coach yelled, the madder and less patient I became.

Looking back on this incident now, I understand what was happening. Smith was a young coach whose leadership hadn't yet taken root as deeply as he would have liked. He was emotional and pissed off from a tough loss and wasn't handling it well. I certainly wasn't helping matters. It wasn't necessarily his fault. He was inexperienced and new on the job. Meanwhile, many of the players followed me; looked to me for guidance and encouragement. By taking me down a notch, Coach was only trying to assert himself and gain control of his team. I get that dynamic now. But when you're nineteen years old and someone's screaming at you in front of your teammates, it's hard to consider the other guy's perspective. Instead, I let my anger get the best of me. As Coach continued to berate me, I jumped to my feet and stormed away toward the dugout.

"Cassidy, come back here! I'm not done with you!" he shouted.

I kept going because I was afraid that if I went back, I was going to whip his ass.

"You get back here right now!" he yelled.

Dude's pushing his luck right now . . . *just keep walking . . . gotta get out of here . . .*

"You get back here or your scholarship is over!"

I don't know who he thought was going to turn around to face him, but it was not going to be a lap dog begging for forgiveness with its tail between its legs. It was going to be a pit bull ready to bite his face off. God, I didn't want that to happen. I kept walking.

"That's it, Cassidy! Get the hell off my team! Take your uniform off! You're outta here!"

At that the pit bull arrived. I spun around and bolted toward him, ripping my jersey off as I ran and throwing it at his feet. In an instant we were nose-to-nose. I could see in his eyes that he was scared and was not prepared to deal with the person I had become at that moment. In my mind the damage was done; he had taken my scholarship and awakened the beast. One of the biggest double-edged swords in my life is my level of commitment. Just like in junior high when I had to either walk away or fight everyone—once I decided to fight, I was all in. I became the momma bear protecting her cubs, completely committed to go as far as it took no matter what the consequences, physically or otherwise. Not too many people in life can get to that level of commitment. It's easy for the bear. They don't have a conscience holding them down; they rely solely on their evolutionary makeup. If we turn the human side of our brain off and tap into the similar evolutionary, animalistic nature of our being, it can greatly simplify a moment in time and can free us from the chains of higher intelligence. Like the bear though, we do this at the peril of all else. It's both freeing and terrifying. Completely freeing in that moment and completely terrifying when looking back at yourself.

Now HE had a decision to make. It was his turn to walk away or go all in, and I could see in his eyes that he'd never seen the level of "all in" that was staring him in the face. Unfortunately, he didn't take the high road. He timidly pushed up closer to me. A split second later I had thrown him to the ground and was moving in to finish him off. Luckily before I could get on top of him, three of my teammates tackled me. Coach Smith scurried away. At the opposite end of the field was my dad trying to climb the fence to get to me, and the crowd in the stands was on their feet, watching this spectacle.

Now I was the bear who was unable to save her cubs and I lashed out at everything around me because of it. There was a guttural need to release the emotions trapped inside me. Again, at the peril of all else.

I was throwing my teammates around, not fighting them but struggling against them as they wrangled to hold me back and shouted at me to calm down. Eventually I was present enough to no longer pursue the coach. I shook free and barreled into the dugout where I spent a good few minutes beating up every object I could find. I threw the water cooler, kicked the catcher's mask and the bubble gum bucket, punched the bat bag, and threw batting helmets around like grenades. It was as if all of the bottled-up emotions I'd kept buried inside all of my life erupted to the surface. The things I compartmentalized, the emotions I swallowed, and the detachment as a defense mechanism I practiced for years all came at a cost. I was very good at ignoring it, but unlike my What bucket that had holes in the bottom and leaked on the ground and away from me, these things were apparently leaking inside of me and building. They were lying dormant but not dead for many years. At this point my tantrum wasn't about the coach, the game, the disrespect, or anything that happened that day, it was just raw emotion that needed to be released from my soul. It was not pretty, it was not fun to watch, and I am not proud of it. When I was all out of rage the only thing left was sadness. Sadness that I hadn't let myself feel for too many years.

Like I said, this was an away game, so we now had to travel back home together. Within a few moments my teammates and the coaching staff were streaming onto the bus with their heads down, taking their seats in silence. Nobody spoke for the duration of the trip home. I've never been on a bus as quiet as that one.

The next day I got a visit from a teammate whom Coach had tapped to play mediator. He told me not to come to practice for the next couple of days, to take some time to cool off and then come in for a meeting with Coach at mid-week. I thought this sounded promising. It sounded to me like Coach was going to apologize for pushing me around and kicking me off the team. I was prepared to apologize too, of course. I loved my team, and despite what had gone down, I liked Coach Smith. And I sure as hell didn't want to lose my scholarship.

On the appointed day I showed up on time for the meeting in the coach's office. When I walked in, he was sitting at his desk, nice and calm. I was nice and calm, too. He motioned for me to take a seat in a chair on the opposite side of his desk. We sat in awkward silence for a moment, and then Coach leaned forward and looked me in the eye.

"Cass, I want to apologize to you," he said. "I didn't react well the other day and I'm sorry about that."

"Yeah, I'm sorry too, Coach," I replied.

"I understand that you were frustrated. I do. But you didn't have to take it that far. Now, with your talent you shouldn't be playing at a school this small anyway. You should be at a division one school where you'll get the exposure and attention you deserve. Honestly, I don't know why you're here."

"I'm here because I like it here! I like everything about this place."

"I know you do, Cass. I know. But unfortunately, you're going to have to make other arrangements. I can't have you back on the team."

"What are you talking about, can't have me back on the team? Yes, you can! Coach, listen . . . I'll run laps. All the laps you want. You can bench me a few games, no problem! I'll write a letter of apology to you and the team, and I'll read it out loud and I'll tell them that you're the coach and I'm just a player and I was wrong to challenge you. I'll cross all the t's and dot all the i's you want me to, but this is my team. I want to be a part of it!"

Coach Smith then reached inside his chest and laid his heart on the table.

"Kevin, here's the bottom line," he said with a heavy sigh. "If I let you back on this team after what happened the other day, I will never be able to get my authority back. Those guys will never see me as a leader again. You and I both know that when a team doesn't respect its leader, it's destined to fail. Surely you can understand that."

Truth be told, I didn't understand that. I still don't. I believe Coach Smith could have salvaged his reputation and kept me on at the same time. However, he would not change his mind. It was official. I was ousted from the team.

I did finish out the semester academically and made many great memories with my friends on the baseball team as well as the guys from the football frat. I'm still friends with a lot of those guys to this day. And I'm proud to say that the following year when I was no longer at that school, all the sacrifices Adam and I made to be baseball players *and* TKEs paid off. The Montagues and Capulets were dead and a new age of judging someone based on Who they are instead of What team they were on began on both sides. I know the following year another baseball player joined, and before the actual frat house got bulldozed (for most likely fair enough reasons) the entire oil and water vibe of the baseball and football teams was gone.

As I've said before, I have always embraced this philosophy of Who over What but was never able to articulate it. As I write this book, I'm constantly reminded how this viewpoint has shaped my character over the years . . . even before I knew what it was. It was as if I had to live it, ponder it, and decode it before I could understand it. These life experiences and many others didn't shape my philosophy as much as they revealed it to me. I lived it before I understood it and I couldn't understand it fully until I was able to sit still long enough to seriously reflect on it.

5

THE EMPTY SEAT IN THE STANDS

Pale sunlight, pale the wall. Love moves away. The light changes. I need more grace than I thought.

—RUMI

JUST AS I HAD DONE SO MANY TIMES IN MY LIFE, I moved on from the disappointment and tried to make the best of my circumstances. Just because Coach Smith had removed one of my planks didn't mean my whole boat was going to sink. I immediately replaced that missing plank by staying at LRU academically for the rest of the semester, making good grades and having fun with my friends. I even thought about playing football there instead of baseball, but I wasn't ready to hang up my baseball spikes just yet. That I had excellent plans for the summer didn't hurt matters: even after learning that I'd been kicked off the LRU squad, the coach for the Maryland Bombers invited me back to play for him in the Clark Griffith League, promising to help me get a scholarship to wherever I wanted to go in the fall. Among a bunch of D-I programs (including our home field at the University of Maryland) he also suggested I consider Brewton-Parker, a smaller college in Georgia well known for developing future pro players. By the time June rolled around, I started to believe that maybe everything would be okay after all. My Bomber teammates chose me as our team captain. We were all living together in an awesome apartment, playing quality ball, and having a lot of fun.

I was sitting in that apartment with a couple of buddies one evening when my mom called unexpectedly.

"I just wanted to let you know that your dad's test results came back today, and he has cancer, but he's going to be fine," she said nonchalantly, her lovable obliviousness in full bloom.

I didn't take this news too hard. Lots of people get cancer and survive. I was sure Dad would come out of it okay. I went about my business, playing ball, goofing around with my friends, talking to college coaches about playing for them in the fall.

But as the summer wore on, the updates on Dad's condition started sounding more dire. In Mom's next call I learned that the reason he had gone to the doctor in the first place was that he was coughing up blood. In other words, he was already super sick by the time they realized there was anything wrong with him. I learned in another call that what had started out as lung cancer had already spread to his liver. Mom remained upbeat as ever, telling me that Dad was just fine and not to worry.

Then came the call where she asked me how my college plans were coming along. I told her I was seriously considering a couple of Mid-Atlantic schools.

"You should probably look for one closer to home," she replied, "so you can be here for your dad."

In that moment reality hit me like a punch in the gut. My dad was not "just fine." He was dying.

• • •

Although my relationship with my father had been a rocky one—especially when I was in my mid-teens—by the time I left for college it had improved greatly. The two of us were getting along well and enjoying each other's company for the first time, largely because Dad was treating me like an adult for a change. He seemed to accept the fact that he'd taught me everything he could and now it was up to me to figure out the rest. I think he enjoyed being the father of adult sons much more than being the father of young boys. Having been the sole disciplinarian in our household, he likely felt 100% responsible for making sure Daniel and I grew up to be decent and productive men. Once we'd graduated high school and moved out of the house, the pressure was off. It must have been a huge relief for him.

Dad even learned to joke around with me, something he'd rarely done when I was a kid. One of my best memories is of the first summer I played baseball in Maryland, when he and Mom came to visit. As they pulled up to the frat house where my teammates and I were staying, I saw that there were empty beer cans strung all over the living room, the fallout from the previous night's party. I scrambled to gather them up but there were too many and it was too late . . . my parents were already on the porch ringing the doorbell. "Dad's going to kill me!" I thought. "Oh well . . ." I took a deep breath and let them in, prepared for all hell to break loose. Just as I feared, Dad's smile quickly disintegrated into an expression of angry disbelief as he looked around the room.

"Oh my God, what is this?" he shouted, picking up a can and shaking it menacingly in my face. "*Lite* beer? What is wrong with you people?" He had a big smile on his face. He was a Budweiser drinker and he didn't have much respect for light beer . . . Ha.

Recalling that moment now, more than twenty years later, I still have trouble coming to terms with the unfairness of it all. Just as I was starting to get along with my old man, he got sick. Very sick. He underwent chemo and a host of other therapies to try to get his Stage 4 cancer under control. It wasn't going well. As summer came to a close, I rushed to find a school near Charlotte with a good baseball program so I could be closer to home. I soon found it: Limestone College in Gaffney, South Carolina, just an hour from my folks. I chose Limestone because it was already on the pro scouts' radar—they'd had a couple guys drafted to the MLB the previous year—and the coach seemed nice. They also had the academic majors I needed. I was planning to be either a teacher or a physical therapist, so my majors were education and pre-med. Limestone was even smaller than LRU, yet not too small. Once there I immersed myself in my studies and fall ball (practice season, essentially), going home every couple of weeks to see my parents.

Every time I went home, Dad's condition was worse. He was still getting up and walking around that fall, but he was getting skinnier by the day. Wasting away, really. At the end of each visit as I headed out to return to school, he'd say, "I'll come to your game next week," and I'd say, "I know you will. I'll see you there." A part of me still believed he might be able to make the trip, but I think deep down we both knew it wasn't going to happen. He was far too weak.

By Christmas he was on home hospice care. They set up a makeshift hospital room for him in what used to be our dining room, the first door on the right after you entered our house. I got to spend a lot of time with him over Christmas break. Daniel was there too, as was the extended family. We spent the majority of our time together pretending Dad was going to come out on the better end of it. It felt almost disrespectful for me to break that barrier of hope (as delusional as it was). When Dad and I were alone we were the unveiled versions of ourselves, talking about things that really mattered. The past and the future. Hopes and dreams. Triumphs, regrets . . . we covered it all. The more we talked the more I liked him.

He made it clear to me that the feeling was mutual. I wish we'd had more times like that because I think we would have been great friends.

Returning to school in January was tough, but the hospice people were taking phenomenal care of Dad. Besides, I knew I'd see him again soon. Over the course of the following months I came home as often as I could.

One February afternoon I walked into the house for a weekend visit. I stepped into the first room on the right to say hello to my dad and found it empty . . . no hospital bed, no medical equipment, no Dad. Nothing. I turned around to find my mom sitting on the couch, crying. My dad had died the day before.

It's a shame that it often takes a tragedy to bring a family closer, but that's what happened with Mom, Daniel, and me. Dad's death brought home the reality of our mortality, which is something we'd never given much thought to (Mom being the carefree type, and Daniel and I still being young enough to believe we'd live forever). Whereas in the past we rarely said "I love you" or hugged each other—it was almost like a business relationship, our family—after Dad died, we became a lot warmer. A lot more affectionate. Our uncles, who'd always been there for us, stepped up even more, calling to check on us often and including us in all their holiday celebrations, especially for the first few years after Dad passed. They were our lifeline.

KEEPING MY HEAD IN THE GAME

I returned to Limestone after Dad's funeral determined to make the most of the remainder of the baseball season, but it was hard. I didn't play my best for a variety of reasons, the most obvious being the loss of my father. I couldn't focus. Ever since I was a little kid I'd been able to look up into the stands and count on seeing my dad, always there, always proud, always cheering me on. Even though I knew that that proud dad only existed in the stands when the distance between us was great enough, deep down it still meant something to me. And looking back after becoming closer to him when I was in college and when he was sick, I realized that that's who he was and was always striving to be. It makes it even sadder looking back on my high school years because we were both the same person trapped on different sides of an unfamiliar world unable to learn the language of the other. The fact that he was not there now and never would be again had a profound effect on me. It felt as if the light in the world had dimmed; like a major star had just tumbled from my galaxy. A star I was just recently aware existed.

When summer rolled around I went back to the Maryland Bombers—once again, a great experience. My baseball scholarship at Limestone was renewed for another year, and I returned to campus with mixed feelings. Happy to be back with my friends but still recovering from losing my dad.

At the beginning of our first practice, the coach called us all into the dugout to go over some housekeeping details, including the election of our team captains for the upcoming season.

"I want you to imagine we're about to go to war," he said. "Now, look around this dugout and ask yourself, *which one of my teammates would I most want beside me in the trenches when the bombs start to drop? Which guy can I trust with my life*?"

We all wrote our choice on a sheet of paper and dropped it in the coach's hat. Myself and two other players had been chosen to lead this team. It felt great to be an official leader of a team and I was excited to get to work on the field.

6

I FOUGHT THE LAW AND THE LAW WON

Not until we are lost do we
begin to understand ourselves.

—HENRY DAVID THOREAU

As the fall semester got into full swing, so did I. I was playing better baseball than I had the previous year; clearly, I was getting my groove back. I felt I still had a decent chance of being drafted by an MLB team, mostly because of my performance in the summer league playing alongside D-I guys, many of whom had already been put in the minor leagues. My studies were going well, too. I had started my student teaching in a sixth-grade classroom, and I was loving it. I always thought I would enjoy teaching and coaching, and this was my first real introduction to it. It was hard but I was a bit of a natural at it. I also got along really well with the teacher in charge of my classroom. She was laid-back and gave me a lot of responsibilities. The kids were pretty good, too.

The only problem I had was a lack of spending money. You can't work full-time when you're on scholarship, so I started picking up odd jobs here and there. I did yard maintenance for the Dean of Academics at his house, and I also worked at the little bar my friends and I liked to go to every week for a couple beers and a game of pool. It was an unofficial job; I'd help the owner bus tables and keep my friends in line, and he'd give me some tip money at the end of the night. Most of the time it was a relaxed place, just like every other place in Gaffney, South Carolina.

I was busy clearing tables at this bar one night when someone stuck their head in the door and yelled that there was a fight in the parking lot. The owner and I ran outside to find a dozen guys involved in a serious brawl. They were really tearing it up. I recognized a few of my baseball teammates among them, and there were also some adult men I didn't know. My boss and I started trying to push and drag people away to break up the fight, but we got pushed and dragged around in return. Pretty soon we were swallowed up by the thrashing crowd. I got hit a few times in the head, the ribs, the back. I could feel blood pouring down my face. It seemed like the fight went on for ten minutes but it was probably only thirty seconds. When I heard police sirens screaming in the distance I thought, "Thank God the cops are coming! I'm getting my butt kicked here!"

No sooner did that thought cross my mind, than I was tackled by a cop and handcuffed. That was okay. I understood that this is how the police break up a fight. Everyone gets handcuffed and separated. Once they'd lined us up with our backs against the parked cars, I was able to get a good look at the group and see that it was made up of half townies and half college guys . . . the typical split for a Saturday night bar fight in a small university town.

A couple of police officers and the bar owner started walking along the line of "suspects" and picking out who could be released and who should go to jail. When they got to me, my boss explained that I worked for him and was involved only because I was helping him break up the fight. The cop shook his head.

"Nope, this one's going to jail," he said. Despite my boss's protests, I was loaded into the back seat of a patrol car and driven to the county's overnight lock up, where I was put into a holding cell with four other guys who'd also been involved in the disturbance. I still wasn't worried. I knew the situation would work itself out. One of my cellmates was released within the hour. A couple hours later another was let go, and then another. The only two left were another baseball player and me. By now we'd been in jail all night, and I was starting to get a little concerned.

Mid-morning a jailer came and took me into a dingy office and sat me down across from a magistrate judge who told me that he was now going to read me my charges.

"Charges? No, there's been a mistake," I said. "You have me mixed up with someone else. See, I work at the bar and I was trying to help my boss break up the . . ."

"Young man, that's enough," said the judge. "This is not the time to plead your case. My only job today is to inform you of the charges against you."

"Okay, please do that then, because I really don't understand what's happening here."

"Mr. Cassidy, you are charged with assault and battery on a law enforcement officer with intent to kill," said the judge in a matter-of-fact tone. "There will be no bail. If convicted of this charge, you're facing twenty-five years to life in prison."

When I heard that, it felt as if all the air was sucked from the room. I could see the judge's lips moving but I didn't hear another word the man said. Next thing I knew I was being helped to my feet by a deputy, handed an orange jumpsuit, and loaded into a squad car for a ride to my new home: the Cherokee County Jail.

NO EASY WAY OUT

Being processed into jail is a surreal experience, especially for someone like me who is the descendant of multiple generations of police officers. Now, to be honest, I've had my share of run-ins with the police in the past but mostly for underage drinking or a party being too loud. Being given the orange jumpsuit like the ones you see on TV was a different level. The deputy who took my fingerprints told me that since I'd been denied bail, I'd probably be in jail for five to seven years before my case even came up for trial.

Back in my cell I looked at the metal bars and the metal bed and the concrete floor and thought, "So this is going to be my life now?" It was such a definitive moment. I had no wiggle room, no options. Accept it or accept it. I literally felt numb. Empty.

Three long days later, a guard came to escort me to a pay phone for an incoming call. It was my Uncle Eddie, the former Harlem cop, calling from his home in Greensboro, North Carolina.

"Kevin, what the hell is wrong with you? What did you do?" he shouted, adding a few other choice words.

"Please listen to me, Uncle Eddie," I said. "All I know is I broke up a fight at the bar where I work, and I've been in jail ever since. I don't know what's happening!"

"I'll tell you what's happening: the article in the newspaper says you beat up a cop and tried to grab his gun, that's what's happening!"

"Uncle Eddie, if you believe that then you should just hang up the phone right now and let me rot in jail. That's not what happened. I'm telling you the truth."

"What does your lawyer say?"

"I don't have a lawyer."

At that Uncle Eddie went ballistic.

"They can't lock you up all this time without legal representation! That's a violation of your rights!"

"I don't think they care about that very much around here," I said.

"Yeah, well I do. I'm coming down there."

Several days passed while Uncle Eddie and my mother (who was out of her mind with worry) scrambled to find me a good defense lawyer. Meanwhile, the bar owner and the teacher under whom I was doing my student teaching were petitioning to get me out of jail because they knew there had to have been a mistake. I had no idea any of this was going on behind the scenes. I was still sitting in jail in my orange jumpsuit, still feeling 100% alone, still thinking I was never getting out.

One day while I was sitting in my cell twiddling my thumbs, a guard came to take me to a conference room where Mom, Uncle Eddie, and my lawyer were waiting to see me. After a round of hugs, we took our seats, and Uncle Eddie slid a newspaper across the table to me. A front-page headline screamed, "Limestone baseball star jailed for attempted murder of police officer" or something to that effect. That's how my family—and the rest of the town—had found out I was in trouble. It was stunning to see it in black and white.

My lawyer explained that he had filed a petition for bail to be set and the judge had granted it. I was going to be released soon. That was a huge relief of course, but there was still the matter of clearing my name. It was going to be my word against the cop who said I'd attacked him. Uncle Eddie and my lawyer had both read the police reports of the incident. They explained that the cop in question was an undercover officer who was outside the bar with another undercover officer when they got into a fight with some college guys. This undercover cop reported that when I jumped into the fray, I tackled him and tried to grab the gun he was carrying in a shoulder holster under his sweatshirt.

"That's a lie!" I said. "I never saw a gun, let alone tried to grab one."

"I know, son. We believe you," Uncle Eddie said. "We've got a good lawyer here and he's doing everything he can to get you out of this mess. The important thing now is to get you out of this *place*."

"That's right," the lawyer said. "And the quickest, surest way to do that is for you to accept a plea deal."

"You mean confess to something I didn't do? Hell no! I have to clear my name. I'm trying to play pro baseball. No scout's going to look twice at me if they think I'm a wannabe cop killer."

"Kevin, if this thing goes to trial it's going to be your word against that of a law enforcement officer, and that would not bode well for you," said the lawyer. "Anything can happen in a trial. Juries find innocent people guilty of crimes all the time. Worst case scenario, you spend the rest of your life in prison."

"He's right," Uncle Eddie said. "Do whatever you have to do to walk out those doors and we'll figure out the rest later."

So that's what I did. I agreed to sign the district attorney's papers. Looking back, the D.A. must have known they had a shell case that could gain publicity because the plea deal consisted of doing community service, having a psychological review, and a few other minor things in return for my record being completely expunged. The only caveat was that I would have to waive my right to sue in the future for defamation of character. Pretty good deal for an official charge of assault and battery with intent to kill a police officer. They put me back in my cell to wait for the court hearing where they would formalize the deal. One day passed . . . two days . . . three days . . . before the hearing took place. The reason it took so long was that the judge was out of town. A lot of legal due process steps were ignored, and my big city police officer uncle didn't make the machine move any faster, as they hated to hear how wrong they were from someone like him. When the judge finally returned, they led me into a courtroom in my orange jumpsuit, shackled from feet to wrists, to approve all the terms of my release.

I was able to walk out of jail that day, but thanks to all the bad press, I lost my student teaching job and my baseball scholarship . . . again. I was able to finish out the school year academically but there would be no baseball season for me. The baseball coach who'd said he wanted a team captain who'd fight in the trenches with him didn't lift a finger to help me when I was in jail and offered no condolences once I was released. I lost a lot of respect for him but was able to use that experience to better identify a person who talked the talk but didn't have the backbone to walk the walk. Like most trials in my life, for some reason or another I didn't take this too hard emotionally, even to the point where a friend who ran the sound system at the baseball field played the song "I Fought the Law and the Law Won" when I stopped by to watch practice one day. I thought it was pretty damn funny. They say you either laugh or cry about hard times and I'm glad I seem to always choose to laugh.

Shortly after I got out of jail, the cop who claimed I tried to kill him was arrested for domestic violence. It was not the first time he'd been accused. The department suspected he might be crooked, so all his cases were flagged for new investigations, including mine. It was determined that the bar fight was started by the two undercover cops, not the college guys. No one at the bar knew they were cops because they were in plain clothes. During the scuffle in the parking lot, the crooked cop's shoulder holster—which no one could see because it was concealed underneath his sweatshirt—got ripped. Instead of just paying the fifty bucks to fix it, he decided to add some spice to his story. As the fight was being broken up, he looked around the parking lot and found the biggest guy in the crowd—Yours Truly—and told the responding officers "the big guy over there" had tried grabbing for his gun, thereby ripping the holster and earning me "intent to kill" on my list of charges.

Although I was told my record was officially "expunged," years later when I had to go through a background check and be fingerprinted for a teaching position, I was crossing my fingers until I finally got the results: all clear. No record. *Whew!*

Looking back, I'm not sure my character was ever tested more than when I was sitting in that jail cell with no hope of returning to normal life. Luckily, I did get to, but those first few days in jail with no contact with the outside world, surrounded by hardened criminals and told that best case I was going to be in there five to seven years then facing twenty-five to life with no other options, all hope was lost. I felt similar to when my father was so sick it was obvious he didn't have much time left but we couldn't admit that out loud. We existed day to day on the surface of reality but not inside of it. That's how I coped in jail. It was a great short-term plan, but if I had spent much more time there and been forced to face the depths of that reality, I can't say for sure how I would've handled it. Luckily for me I was released. What I was in that jail was inmate twenty-three of E block and hopefully my Who would have been strong enough to get me through that life. I'm glad I'll never know, though. What it did do for me was put life in perspective. It is a lot easier to treat some of life's challenges as small or trivial once you've had that jail cell door slammed in your face. That experience sure toughened me up, but I found out later in life it was also a key factor in my lack of empathy. Something that, once identified, I have had to consciously work on.

NEW COLLEGE, NEW LEAGUE

After all the upheaval and uncertainty of the previous school year, I was never more ready to return to my anchor, my salvation: the summer baseball league in Maryland. I was welcomed back with open arms for what would be my final summer season. I played really well that summer. Again, my coach suggested I look into attending Brewton-Parker College, the "baseball factory" school in Georgia that he'd been trying to get me to go to for years. This time I agreed as my options were very limited. I have no idea why though . . . after trying to beat up one coach then being arrested for attempted murder, you'd think I was exactly what every D-I school was looking for! HA! Even after all that, based on the word of my summer coach (my Who coming to my rescue again!) I was awarded a scholarship to Brewton-Parker and went on to have a great year and made it to the NAIA World Series in Idaho.

As the season drew to a close, the Brewton-Parker coach was able to get me a professional contract with an independent baseball league, which is the equivalent of Major League Baseball's Single-A level except it's not owned by an MLB franchise. In other words, playing in this league is like being a professional free agent. You can be picked up by any MLB team at any time. It's baseball at the second-highest level, essentially. I did very well and was invited back to play for another year, but I hesitated. At twenty-three, I was already considered old in the baseball world. While I was busy getting kicked out of schools and going to jail, all my teammates from the Maryland summer league and several more from college had been drafted and were playing minor league ball. All of these guys were excellent players but they were telling me horror stories about all the hardships and frustrations with the business side of baseball, and it wasn't very encouraging. Stories of teammates who were in their early thirties with wives and kids, still making no money, still living with host families, looking for entry level jobs in the off season. Stories of others who were literally sitting on the bench while high school kids who'd been signed for five million were getting more playing time than they were. Those kids were going to play no matter what because the team had invested big money in them. Meanwhile, excellent older players were being sent to the outfield to shag balls for the young "superstars."

I knew what page I was on. No team had invested in me. No team was going to give me the benefit of the doubt. I was a fine player, but unless I got exponentially better overnight, I was not going to make it all the way to the top. As I weighed my options, I had to admit that the MLB didn't seem like a realistic goal anymore. I'd hitched a ride on the baseball train for as long as I could and had a blast doing it, but it was time to get my life going. I hung up my baseball cleats forever and returned home to Charlotte to take stock of my options.

LIFE LESSONS LEARNED

Going through the trauma of my arrest and incarceration and the fallout from it—most notably the derailing of my baseball career—was critical to my character development. The experience confirmed yet again that whatever role I'm assigned to play in any given moment (a What), whether it's "baseball player" or "accused felon," is not Who I am at my core. Still, my identity as a baseball player was extremely important to me. Sometimes people use identity as a crutch, which is not always a bad thing. There were times in my life when baseball served as a crutch to get me through the hard times and give me an outlet. Crutches are great; they help you when you have a broken leg and need something to lean on, but they're not meant to be used forever. You need to know when to throw that thing down and walk on your own again. In other words, you can identify to some extent as a What to get you through difficulty, but only if you don't get so attached to it that you can't leave it.

The derailing of my baseball career was critical to my character development. The experience confirmed yet again that whatever role I'm assigned to play in any given moment (a What), whether it's "baseball player" or "accused felon,"

IS NOT WHO I AM AT MY CORE.

My brush with the law also showed me who my true friends were . . . and who they weren't. Turns out I had a ton of good friends who were determined to make me laugh and feel better about myself. They helped me move forward.

That doesn't mean I didn't struggle. A few weeks after I got out of jail and wasn't allowed back on the baseball team, I started feeling overwhelmed emotionally. My friends and family encouraged me to talk about it, but I found that the more I dwelled on the disappointment the bigger and more powerful it became, like its own self-fulfilling prophecy. It reminds me of when my dad died. I didn't cry for a week afterward, and when I did, it was in the car by myself during the drive back to school. Every time I talked about Dad's death the pain enveloped me like a thick fog. It lingered and gave me an excuse to wallow in my loss. More than that, it gave me a reasonable excuse to be less and to do less. It was an excuse that everyone had to accept. For me it has been much more efficient to just keep moving forward and only look back on the negative experiences occasionally for a recap of what I've learned. Doing so keeps me centered on the lessons and the solutions, not on the problem.

Listen up, because this is important. *When you focus your attention on something, it expands. It gets bigger.* Focus on problems, you get more problems. Focus on solutions, you get more solutions.

My wife, Megan, and I were listening to a podcast recently in which a woman called in for help because she was tired all the time. Tired from raising little kids, tired from starting a new business, tired from running a household, etc. The longer she talked, the more exhausted she sounded. The more positive reinforcement she got from the show's host, the more she dwelled on being tired. I couldn't stand it. I turned to Megan and said I had an easy fix for that caller.

WHEN YOU FOCUS YOUR ATTENTION ON SOMETHING, IT EXPANDS. IT GETS BIGGER.

"It's simple: she needs to stop talking about how tired she is," I said. "Labeling herself as 'tired' has become a self-fulfilling prophecy for her. Even when she's not tired she'll probably convince herself that she is, or should be. And the more sympathy she gets for being tired, the more she'll play that card . . . even if it's only subconsciously."

Want to stop feeling tired (or stressed, or unappreciated, or lonely, or disappointed)? Stop talking about it all the time! Shift your focus away from your perceived deficit and aim it toward cultivating whatever it is you want more of in your life. If you're feeling tired, for example, train yourself to spot the moments when you're feeling even the slightest bit energetic and talk about *that.* Celebrate it, feel gratitude for it, and watch it increase. What you focus on is what will grow and that will be what's ultimately projected out into the world. Even deeper than that is how you talk to yourself. What you say inside your own mind can literally change your perception of a situation. Ultramarathon runner, entrepreneur, and famous motivational speaker Jesse Itzler often talks about his experiences with "positive self-talk," as he puts it. He has tricked his mind from being physically tired during a race to becoming energized just by telling himself, "I feel great" instead of "I feel tired." For him, and I have experienced this as well, positive self-talk has enabled him to run longer and push past fatigue. If it can do that to physical barriers imagine what it can do for mental ones!

Our perception of the world creates the world around us, not the other way around. It sounds crazy but it's true. If you can wrap your mind around that fact and implement positive self-talk every time you start to convince yourself that you are tired or stressed or overwhelmed, you'll be amazed how fast it can change your life. When you hear yourself say, "I'm tired," learn to catch yourself and say, "I feel great" instead. It's that simple. Soon it will become a habit and eventually it can become your default. Soon everyone around you will be saying, "I want what that guy is having!"

7

MOVING TO THE HEAD OF THE CLASS

He allowed himself to be swayed by his conviction that human beings are not born once and for all on the day their mothers give birth to them, but that life obliges them over and over again to give birth to themselves.

—GABRIEL GARCÍA MÁRQUEZ, *LOVE IN THE TIME OF CHOLERA*

LEAVING BASEBALL AND GOING BACK HOME to Momma wasn't the most empowered feeling I've ever had, but it wasn't devastating, either. I needed time to get my feet on the ground and figure out what to do next, and Mom's house was as good a place as any to get that done. The rent was free, the food was free, and the motherly advice was free, too.

Mom's preference was that I follow through on becoming a teacher and a coach. I had my education degree and I already knew I enjoyed the work thanks to my student teaching experience. Mom was right. Going into education made sense. I started looking around Charlotte for a teaching job.

But one night I went out for a beer with Josh, my best friend growing up, and he threw a wrench into my best laid plans. He explained that he was getting ready to move to a town outside Baltimore to be closer to a girl he was dating.

"Remember how you and I always talked about moving somewhere together after college?" he said. "Well, how about now? Come up to Baltimore with me. I need a roommate and you need to get out of your mom's house. My girlfriend says there's plenty of work up there. What do you think?"

It took me less than five seconds to decide.

"I got nothing else to do," I said. "Let's go to Baltimore."

SCHOOL DAYS

Josh and I moved into a nice little apartment in Ellicott City, a suburb of Baltimore, and I got busy figuring out what I was going to do next. I tried a sales job for a brief time—long enough to realize it wasn't something I wanted to do for the rest of my life—and had fun hanging out with Josh, his girlfriend, Holly, and her roommates. In a bit of sweet serendipity, Holly was an elementary school teacher outside D.C. I told her I'd always wanted to teach and coach and even had a degree in education, and she said she'd look into getting me an interview in her school district. Turns out they were hiring (more serendipity!). Holly put in a good word for me and got me fast-tracked through the hiring process. I ended up getting a job at the middle school that her elementary school fed into. The commute was long and the school was in a shady part of town, but I liked it. I was making around $25,000 a year—good money, for me—but still not a lot to live on. The old car I'd been driving broke down, so I bought a modest used car and had to make payments on that in addition to my share of the rent and utilities. I also got my first credit card and started using it to pay for dinner and drinks with friends. I was always able to make the payments, but some debt started piling up. It was not the most responsible thing I've ever done, not by a long shot. This debt would end up becoming a big problem for me later on, but I don't want to get too far ahead of myself here . . .

I loved my teaching job. The principal was really cool, and all the teachers I worked with were supportive. It was obvious they were there for the right reason: they wanted to make life better for the kids, many of whom lived in a group home or were being raised by grandparents and didn't have many, if any, positive role models around. Being with my colleagues in this environment reminded me a lot of being on a sports team. I fit in from Day One. Mom came to visit a few times and was so proud that I was doing something positive with my life . . . finally.

There were definitely challenges in this work though, as any teacher can tell you. At this particularly rough school it was mostly behavior. Aggression, drugs, and broken homes were the norm. I did my best to help as many kids as I could, but you learn pretty fast that you can't save them all. The best thing about this school was the administration, headed by the principal. She and I were on the same philosophical page. Tough love, with an emphasis on the tough *and* the LOVE.

A few months after I started this job, Josh and Holly got engaged and made plans to move in together, so I moved in with a friend of a friend from the rec basketball league we played in. Even though his apartment was in a less-than-stellar neighborhood, I loved it there. I continued to play rec ball, hang out with friends, and commute to D.C. every day to teach. On weekends we'd go out and have a few beers and return to the apartment to watch late night TV until it was time to crash. One of our favorite things to watch was a wild sport called SlamBall. If you're not familiar with it, it's like a cross between basketball, football and Cirque du Soleil. It's played on a modified basketball court that has four big trampolines embedded in the floor on both ends, a springy cushioned floor in between, and tall plexiglass walls all around, as in hockey. Players from opposing teams try to score like in basketball, but thanks to the trampolines they can bounce and literally fly through the air, achieving crazy heights. And as in hockey, players can block and collide with their opponents to prevent them from scoring. I learned that the creator of SlamBall envisioned it being like a live action video game, and in my mind, he achieved his vision. It truly is insane to see enormous guys soaring over the court like birds, slamming into each other and dunking the ball from high above the rim. Whenever I watched it on TV with my friends, someone would always say that I would have been a great SlamBall player. With all that hard-hitting action, it was right up my alley.

One day I got an email from a friend, Brian, telling me he'd seen an advertisement for a SlamBall tryout in Philadelphia in a couple of weeks. He informed me that we were going to drive up there, hang out for the weekend, and go to the tryouts. And if I had any objections, too bad. He'd already signed me up.

FLYING HIGH

When we arrived for the tryouts, which were held at Temple University's basketball arena, we found the gymnasium's foyer crammed with registration tables and tons of young guys like me who'd seen SlamBall on TV and decided to give it a shot. After completing the paperwork, we were told to go into the gym and sit in the stands, which soon filled with hundreds of other wannabe SlamBall stars, mostly guys between the ages of eighteen and thirty who thought they could have been a pro athlete at some point and were there to give it one more shot. I was there just for fun. I wasn't really taking it seriously until Pat Croce, then-owner of the Philadelphia 76ers, took the court to give the welcoming speech. I had no idea that Croce, a sports legend, was heavily involved in the SlamBall world. It was then I realized that this tryout was legit.

After Croce's speech the organizers separated us into groups and put us through a series of athletic drills on the court. In addition to regular ball handling, we had to dribble a basketball while taking football-style hits with arm pads the coaches wore. My kind of fun. Just as quickly as they got us on the court, they started cutting people. As with any sports endeavor, if 1,000 people show up to play, 800 of them are going to be delusional about how good they are. They were soon dismissed. Out of the 200 who remained, only 30 were identified as potential SlamBall material. I was one of them. At the end of the weekend I was invited to travel to Los Angeles for the next level of tryouts, all expenses paid.

Now I had a decision to make: do I go forward with this crazy SlamBall thing or return to the safe, respectable confines of my classroom? I didn't see how I could do both. As soon as I got to school on Monday morning I went to my principal and laid it all out for her. I told her that I'd been invited to LA for a SlamBall tryout that would last two weeks. At any point during that time they could cut me and send me home, but if I made it I'd have to stay there for the rest of the year.

"If going to LA will cause me to burn this bridge as a teacher, I'm not going to do it," I explained to her. "But if I knew I could come back and still have my job if I get cut, I'd really like to give it a shot. I don't know . . . what do you think?"

"Are you kidding me?" she said. "Absolutely, you should go! You'll always have a job here. Go get 'em!"

Sweet! The only thing left to do now was break the news to my mother. As I expected, she flipped. She couldn't believe I was putting my stable, productive life on hold to run off to LA . . . to do what? To try to maybe play a sport that no one had ever heard of? To risk being a loser again?

I laughed and reassured her that I'd probably be cut within a week, at which point I'd return to my classroom as if nothing had ever happened. No harm, no foul . . . and I'd have enjoyed a free trip to California.

8

CITY OF DREAMS

A ship in harbor is safe, but that is not
what ships are built for.

—JOHN A. SHEDD

UPON ARRIVAL IN LA, I joined 200 other SlamBall hopefuls in the hotel that would be our home for the duration of our stay. These were men who'd made the initial cut in tryouts across the country just like the one I'd attended in Philadelphia. They put us two to a room; I was happy to learn that my roommate was a guy I'd met at the Philly tryout. Otherwise, I didn't know anyone else there. Every day we'd go play ball—every day was an audition, so to speak—and every evening we'd return to the hotel for barbecuing and beers. It was a lot of fun but there was pressure, too. Several times a week the organizers would cut a handful of players by calling their hotel room in the evening and telling them that their SlamBall days were over before they'd even begun. We'd wake up the next morning to find a couple more guys gone. Every night we'd wait for our phone to ring and hope like hell it didn't.

I never got one of those calls. I was among 100 players chosen for the draft, but even then we were not guaranteed a spot on a team. Only thirty new players would make that ultimate cut. Sitting in the draft room was pretty surreal. It wasn't as big and fancy as the NFL draft but it did have many of the same bells and whistles. A big stage with a podium looking out over the crowd, and a huge draft board on the back wall of the stage outlining who had been picked by whom and what picks were coming up next. To add to the drama the MC announcing each pick would do so in way that teased who the pick was. Something like, "This West Coast player who the scouts immediately identified as a highflyer was the perfect fit. With his basketball background and a willingness to go the extra mile during this grueling tryout process, the Chicago Mob select John Doe with the third pick of the first round." Then John Doe would walk up to the podium, shake the MC's hand, meet his new coach, pose for pictures, and receive a round of applause. It was all pretty cool.

The best part is that every player in the room had become friends at this point because we were all living at the same hotel and had been on one big tryout team for the last few weeks. With every pick people were genuinely happy but at the same time a little worried because that was one less pick left for them to be drafted. Luckily, I was drafted by a team called The Mob in the fourth round out of twelve, so I was able to relax and enjoy myself much more than the guys drafted in the twelfth round . . . or not at all. When I walked up to that stage, shook my coach's hand, and posed for pictures, for a brief few seconds I allowed myself to think, "I've made it!"

Back at the hotel I phoned my principal and said I wouldn't be returning to school. It was a bittersweet conversation. I was excited about making the team, of course, but I couldn't stop thinking about my students. I asked the principal to please tell them I missed them and would never forget them. She assured me that she would and reiterated that the door would always be open if I ever wanted to come back. She closed the call by saying that she was genuinely happy for me and couldn't wait to see me on TV.

Then I called my mom, who had the opposite reaction. Really, at this point who could blame her?

GOOD TIMES!

In the four months following the draft, my teammates and I practiced in a warehouse that had been converted into a SlamBall training facility. We were lodged at the Safari Inn, a U-shaped two-story hotel with all the rooms opening onto a swimming pool and a grilling area in the middle. It was there that my fellow SlamBallers and I continued our nightly tradition of barbeque and beers. We had a blast together. I was one of the smaller players in the league; many of the guys stood 6'8 and up. Our room and board were paid in full and we each received a per diem of around $1,000 a month. We weren't making any money to speak of, but we had everything we needed, including the most important thing of all: *hope*. We knew that if this sport took off and did well on television, we could become stars. After all we were in LA and this is where stars are born!

Although the training lasted three months, the actual season would last only one month. Short but intense: we would play one game a night on four consecutive nights every week at the SlamBall stadium located just outside Universal CityWalk Hollywood. Our games were to be taped and televised six months later.

Finally, the night of our first real game arrived. Instead of driving to that dingy warehouse in Burbank where we'd spent the previous three months practicing and scrimmaging against each other, three other players and I were now driving to Hollywood, more specifically to Universal CityWalk. I had never been there before so I had no idea what to expect. My first introduction to the scale of the place was as we were pulling into the park. If you have never been there before, it's similar to getting into Disney World.

The first thing you do is drive through a check-in gate, pay for parking, and get maps . . . not just maps of the property but of all the different parking decks as well. We had our players' passes and were quickly pointed to our parking deck with a map that would take us to the stadium. My three teammates and I were trying to figure this out like it was an episode of *The Amazing Race.* Universal CityWalk includes Universal Studios, a huge movie production lot, an amusement park with live shows and studio tours, as well as a big boardwalk-type place filled with shops, restaurants, a movie theater, and street performers. Just inside this boardwalk area, close to the main entrance of the studio lot, stood our destination: a 5,000-seat SlamBall stadium.

When my teammates and I finally completed our *Amazing Race* challenge and found the stadium, we were in awe. We'd arrived several hours before game time so workers were still milling around setting up and organizing, but I think all of us could picture that stadium full of screaming fans. It was an awesome, exhilarating feeling.

We got to do some warmups and try out the new court before any spectators were allowed inside. Then we went to our locker rooms located in big circus tents erected outside the stadium for meetings, rehab, ankle taping, etc. When we finally came out to enter the stadium hours later the sun had gone down, the lights were on, and there was a line of people around the park to get in. Suddenly this SlamBall thing became very real and that's when the nerves kicked in. We went on the court for our pre-game warmups at the same time as they were letting people into the stadium. It was hard to concentrate on the court with so many fans piling into the seats. There was an MC on a microphone and cheerleaders hyping the place up. The energy from the crowd soon spilled onto the court and the excitement was palpable. I went from nervous to exhilarated very quickly.

We had to run back into the tents after warmups as the cheerleaders and MC kept the crowd going. We heard everything from in there and were able to see it, too, as the TV feed was broadcast on closed circuit TVs for us in the tent. The teams waiting to play next could watch the game in progress, and the teams that had just finished could hang out, heal up, and watch the next game in there as well.

The sidelines in SlamBall are like hockey benches right up next to the playing floor, and as the starting lineups were called out, we jumped the half wall and ran out on the court to standing ovations. The opening tip off was electric, but when the ball was in play, all of us players found ourselves right back in that warehouse, laser focused on the game. The game moves fast and the hits are relentless, but there are enough breaks in the game that we could look up and acknowledge the crowd and take it all in every once in a while. Many of these SlamBall players had played football or basketball in front of tens of thousands of people and even up to 100,000 in their college days, so the numbers weren't staggering to us, but the energy was. The fans here were up-close and personal, banging on the glass like in hockey.

I'd compare it to a musician playing a concert at a huge stadium versus a smaller, more intimate venue. The pressure is more tangible in smaller venues because you can see the fans' faces. You connect with them and feel responsible for making sure you deliver to each and every one of them as opposed to one huge faceless crowd. There was little to no chance the fans were not going to get what they came for. The sport sells itself and the players are legit athletes going all out.

We played well enough to get the win that night and supplied plenty of footage for the highlight reel. After the game we signed autographs and mingled with the crowd a bit. This would become our routine every Thursday, Friday, Saturday, and Sunday for four weeks straight. As the season went on it was really special to see a lot of the same faces in the crowd night after night, and soon some of us players got nicknamed, heckled, and cheered for. I ended up with two nicknames: "The Lumberjack" and "The Beast" . . . both compliments to how I was playing. It didn't take long before I began to hear the crowd chanting "Beast! Beast! Beast!"—none more enthusiastically than when a couple of my high school friends came to one of my games. I played well that night, and every time I made a great play, they would start the chant that the rest of the crowd happily joined. It was awesome!

Meanwhile, my mom was back in North Carolina having what Southern folks call a "conniption fit." She was terrified that something bad would happen to me in out in LA where we had no family or friends. She had learned to be okay with not checking in on me daily and one time even said, "I don't want to know all the crazy things you're doing. Just let me know you're still alive once a week, please." She was as supportive as she could be from a distance, but I think she needed to see exactly what I was up to in LA. When the practice season ended and the games started, she asked if she could come out to watch me play. Against my better judgment, I said yes. SlamBall is a full contact sport with broken noses, fractured limbs, and dislocated fingers happening practically every game. It's like football times 1,000. Mom could barely watch me finish a BMX race when I was a kid and definitely looked away most of my football career. I wasn't sure she would be able to handle watching me get banged around like that but clearly, she needed to see me for her own peace of mind. She was trying to be supportive, so I felt like I had to let her come.

I was relaxing in my room the day Mom arrived at the Safari Inn by taxi from the airport. She walked into the middle of the hotel complex to find half a dozen giant men grilling burgers by the pool. She froze, thinking that perhaps she was in the wrong place. One of my most massive teammates spotted her standing there like a statue, eyes as big as the moon.

"Can I help you, ma'am?" he asked.

"Kevin Cassidy . . . my son?" she stammered. "I'm looking for him . . ."

"Oh my God, y'all!" he shouted to the others. "It's Cass's mama!"

Within seconds my mom was surrounded, picked up, bear hugged, and carried to a nearby picnic table where she was gently set down and given a burger hot off the grill. Meanwhile, one of the guys came up to fetch me. I arrived downstairs to find her encircled by my teammates, smiling, giggling, and having a ball.

Mom didn't seem too worried about me in LA after that.

I played the entire season of SlamBall and did well, becoming one of the sport's most visible players. I did radio interviews in the six-month gap leading up to the show's debut on Spike TV, and my image was chosen to be featured on SlamBall press releases for the following year. It was all very exciting except for one problem . . . when the SlamBall season ended, so did the room and board and per diem payments. I did odd jobs with the goal of staying in LA until the next season began, but I couldn't make it. I was broke, and not only broke but $10,000 in debt thanks to that credit card I'd started running up in Baltimore. I also fell behind on my car payment.

I hid this sad truth from my mother because I didn't want her to worry, and I certainly didn't want to hear her say, "I told you so." Besides, there was nothing she could do about it. It wasn't as if she was rolling in money and could afford to help me. As much as I hated to leave LA, I returned to Baltimore to tread water until SlamBall called me back.

CHARM CITY REDUX

I arrived in Baltimore penniless, homeless, and jobless, but I did have one big thing going for me. I had awesome friends. My buddy Brian—the same guy who went to the SlamBall tryout with me in Philly—and his wife, Andrea, were kind enough to take me in and set me up on their sofa for the time being. Now that I had a roof over my head, I could turn my attention to putting some cash in my pocket. I knew I could return to my old teaching job outside Washington D.C., but I didn't want to go through the trauma of having to leave my students again when the time came to head back to SlamBall. I decided that the best strategy was to substitute teach during the day and bartend at night. Another friend helped me get a substitute teaching position at the middle school where he worked, and yet another buddy gave me a part-time job at his bar.

Even with all my friends' help, I continued to spiral downward financially. I couldn't make enough money to pay my car loan, insurance, and credit card payment, let alone get an apartment of my own. I hated having to rely on Brian and Andrea for my every need. When my car was repossessed and I was left without transportation to get to and from work, I knew it was time to swallow what little pride I had left and call Mom.

As you might imagine, she was not happy to hear of my situation. We decided that she'd drive up to Baltimore to get me and take me back to Charlotte. When she arrived at the house, she didn't even come inside to say hello to Brian and Andrea, let alone thank them for feeding and lodging me for months. I said goodbye to them and climbed into Mom's van with the only possession I had left, a bag of clothes. The drive to North Carolina was a chilly one, I can promise you that.

My plan was to stay with my mother just long enough to find a job and save up the money to move into my own place . . . but you can probably guess how it actually turned out. I lasted only a week at Mom's house. I couldn't handle my shame at having to be there. I got on a Greyhound bus and went back to Baltimore and Brian's couch.

As difficult as this episode was, it was a time of great character building for me as a young man. I learned a lot about fiscal restraint, most notably that debt is really, *really* bad. It enslaves you, takes away your freedom and your dignity. Being able to delay gratification is what it's all about. There's a good book on that topic that I think everybody, especially teenagers, should read. It's called *Don't Eat the Marshmallow—Yet! The Secret to Sweet Success in Work and Life* by Ellen Singer and Joachim de Posada. It's a corny little book but it teaches an important life lesson. It's based on a study done at Stanford University in the 1970s in which researchers brought children one by one into a room, put a marshmallow on the table in front of them, and told them that they could either eat that marshmallow now or wait fifteen minutes and get two. The researchers then left the room and returned fifteen minutes later to find out which choice the child had made. Some had been unable to resist the temptation and gobbled up their marshmallow right away. Others had waited patiently for their double reward. The researchers recorded the results and ten years later went back to the same kids to see how they were doing. They analyzed their SAT scores and other educational markers as well as other indicators of "success" and found that the children who'd had the willpower to wait for the second marshmallow had better outcomes later on.

Don't Eat the Marshmallow turns this research into an easy-to-read parable that really drives home the notion that patience and self-control pay off in the long run. I wish that book had been around when I was younger. Maybe reading it would have saved me some trouble. Then again, maybe not. Sometimes it's best to learn the hard way, because the more painful the lesson, the more it sticks with you. These days if I want something but don't yet have the money for it in my bank account, I'm not having it. I never want to feel the way I felt during this hard chapter of my life. I believe that even if you aren't born with a lot of self-discipline, you can develop it with the right training and support. You can make it part of your enduring—and much healthier—Who. I'm living proof of that. Truth be told if I had kept a decent job the debt wouldn't have piled up. What I needed was to come to grips with the type of person I was. At that point in my life, I knew damn well I wasn't stable enough financially to put things on credit cards and should've been harder on myself than I was about that fact. I could almost physically see my parents throwing their hands in the air and saying, "I guess he'll just have to learn the hard way" again.

Someone once told me that if you're gonna be stupid, you better be tough. I've always liked that saying and feel my toughness has bailed me out of some stupid mistakes. Another saying I like is "Fool me once, shame on you, fool me twice, shame on me." I take this to heart and make sure I don't make the same mistake twice. Instead, I think I find completely new mistakes to make. Life's path is full of making mistakes, but learning from them is what strengthens your Who. When my parents were no longer able to gift me with the freedom to fail, life stepped up and kept on delivering that package to my doorstep! If you're free enough to fail, make sure you're smart and humble enough to learn from it. It is nearly impossible to formulate a strong Who without humility. Humility, among other things, is the ability to blame yourself in a healthy way in order to grow. If you can't shoulder the blame, you can't cultivate the growth.

I BELIEVE THAT EVEN IF YOU AREN'T BORN WITH A LOT OF SELF-DISCIPLINE, YOU CAN DEVELOP IT WITH THE RIGHT TRAINING AND SUPPORT.

DECISIONS, DECISIONS . . .

Back on Brian's sofa, I took stock of my situation. I thought long and hard about what to do next. I certainly didn't want to remain semi-homeless, that's for sure . . . but honestly, I didn't know how to get myself out of this mess. I knew I didn't want to teach full-time only to have to leave my students when SlamBall called. Even if I could manage to scrape together rent money doing part-time work like substitute teaching, bartending, and personal training, I was afraid to commit to a roommate or sign a lease because I'd only have to break it off to return to California. Brian and Andrea assured me that I was welcome to hang out with them until my situation got settled, but I felt so guilty taking up space in their living room again.

And then I got the call I'd been waiting for. It was the SlamBall people, but the news they delivered wasn't what I wanted to hear. While they assured me that they were in the process of returning for another season, the start date had been pushed back due to a creative dispute. SlamBall's inventor/owner had sold part of the rights to Warner Brothers in order to get his sport on TV. Although the show had good ratings and was well-received, Warner Brothers wanted to turn SlamBall into a competition series like *American Gladiators*. The owner pushed back on that because he intended for it to be a real sport, not a reality show. The bottom line: while they were fighting it out in Hollywood, my fellow SlamBallers and I were caught in the middle, in limbo.

I called my good friend Chris in LA to get his take on this new development. Chris, a former Clemson quarterback, was a SlamBall teammate of mine, so he and I were in the same leaky boat in that regard but with one notable difference . . . he had a life raft when it came to off-season employment. When he wasn't playing SlamBall he was busy doing stunt work in sports movies, commercials, and television shows. He listened as I explained my dilemma.

"SlamBall may or may not return," I said. "Meanwhile, I'm sitting here in Baltimore . . ."

"Baltimore?" Chris interrupted. "What are you doing in Baltimore?"

"Substitute teaching, tending bar, stuff like that."

"You can do that here! Come back to LA so you'll be here when SlamBall calls."

"I can't afford to live in LA, man."

"Yes, you can. You can stay with me."

"Chris, I need you to understand that I'm flat broke. I won't be able to contribute anything to your household."

"Not important. Just get here. We'll find something for you to do while we wait for SlamBall."

We'll find something for you to do . . . that was pretty damn vague, but I had to admit that *something in LA* was better than *nothing in Baltimore.* "Now how do I get to LA?" I wondered. At that time I had about $1,000 to my name. I had saved a little as I was living rent free on Brian's couch, but that was going to be gone once I paid off all my debt and I would be back to square one. And most of those bills didn't go toward the principle I owed, but toward the interest that had accrued. Unless I could double my payments there was no way out of this cycle. I did a lot of soul searching and even more research. I felt deep down that going to LA to live on Chris's couch was the right move, sort of a rebirth for me, but I knew I wouldn't be able to breath freely there with no money and lingering debt staring over my shoulder. The debt stood at a staggering $10,000. A huge and insurmountable number for me at that time in my life.

I researched options and found a way out. I'm not proud of this way out as it is not taking responsibility for your actions and came at a cost. My only option was to declare bankruptcy. The cost was the attorney fees and the fact that my credit would go to zero and I would have no borrowing power. That part was kind of a motivating factor for me. I didn't have any borrowing power as it was, but if I was able to live debt free for seven years the bankruptcy would be deleted from my file. It would allow me to breathe freely in California and establish a clear path to financial redemption. A seven-year path, but a path. The lawyer fees took half my money and the flight took the other half, but I was en route to California with only one way to go . . . up.

9

THE DROP KICK SEEN 'ROUND THE WORLD

A cloud does not know why it moves in just such a direction and at such a speed. It feels an impulsion . . . this is the place to go now. But the sky knows the reason and the patterns behind all clouds, and you will know, too, when you lift yourself high enough to see beyond horizons.

—RICHARD BACH

I SETTLED INTO CHRIS'S HOUSE and quickly got some gigs through his and his roommates' connections doing personal training and bartending. Barely scraping by but enjoying the change of scenery, I was happy to be in California. I liked the weather, the vibe, the people I was hanging out with . . . especially Chris and his friends. They were dialed into the world of sports movies, television, and commercials for brands like Nike and EA Sports. This was a world I knew nothing about and I thought it was fascinating. I loved hearing their stories about being on set, meeting celebrities, the ups and downs of stunt work (pun intended). Their jobs were not only interesting and challenging, but some of these guys were making six figures working only a couple days a week. So when Chris mentioned that he knew the guys who were hiring athletes for a new sports movie and asked if I'd like to try for a part in it, he definitely had my attention.

The movie in question was the remake of the Burt Reynolds classic *The Longest Yard*, this time starring Adam Sandler. The original was one of my favorites growing up; I'd seen it probably half a dozen times. It's the story of an incarcerated former pro quarterback (played by Reynolds) who gets pressured by the prison warden to put together a football team made up of fellow convicts to play a game against the guards. When the warden tells Reynolds's character that he'll let him out of prison early if he'll throw the game and allow the guards to win, Reynolds has a decision to make: betray his teammates and take the "get out of jail free" card, or stand up with them and crush the guards on the gridiron. *The Longest Yard* is one of those great underdog stories that everybody loves. Since I was feeling like an underdog myself at this point in my life, the movie seemed like the perfect match for me. There was a hitch, though. The casting director was looking for real football stars—ex-college and NFL players like Chris and his roommates—who also knew their way around a movie set. I did not fit that description. I knew nothing about making movies and hadn't touched a football since high school. Chris and his friend Justin, another stuntman, worked hard to convince me to give it a try.

"You can do this, Cass," Justin said. "Hell, if you can do SlamBall you can *definitely* do this!"

Looking back on this particular decision, it didn't seem like that big a deal at the time—mostly because I didn't have any other options and the worst thing that could happen was ending up back on Chris's couch. Today I am struck by how pivotal that "of course, why not" decision turned out to be. Practically everything I have in my life right now is mine because I said yes to this opportunity. Former Google CEO Eric Schmidt is credited with saying, "Find a way to say yes!" I had absorbed the power of that message long before he came along. Maybe it's because I'm naturally optimistic or maybe it's because I'd read and taken to heart these words from Mark Twain:

> Twenty years from now you'll be more disappointed
> by the things you didn't do than by the ones you did.
> So throw off the bowlines. Sail away from the safe
> harbor. Catch the trade winds in your sails.

EXPLORE. DREAM. DISCOVER.

Whenever you're presented with a new opportunity, I recommend that you look for reasons to say yes rather than no. No = Status Quo. Yes = Endless Possibilities. I choose the Endless Possibilities option whenever I can, and that's why I said yes to moving to Baltimore, yes to teaching, yes to trying out for SlamBall, yes to moving to LA, and yes to this opportunity to try out for my first movie. At this point I had been so many Whats in my life they were white noise, and my Who seemed to be forged out of steel so going to this tryout was a no brainer. The part I needed help with was the self-talk. I needed to be confident and powerful in order to make the team. Deep down I knew this could be my ticket to a financially stable life doing something I enjoyed and was good at. That doesn't happen too many times in life and I was very intimidated by it. For me it seemed almost easier to not try than to get close to it and fail. But Chris and his roommates, who quickly became friends of mine, made my self-talk and self-doubt irrelevant. They weren't having it and they provided the confidence boost I needed to be able to show up with the right attitude and best chance for success.

The tryouts for *The Longest Yard* were a lot like the ones I did for SlamBall. As I said in the introduction, I had to show up to a big auditorium, fill out paperwork, talk to the hiring coaches, and see if I was good enough on paper to even attend the tryout. SlamBall on my resume was the only reason I got the invite. At the tryout I was surrounded by guys who had played for some of the best college teams in the nation as well as several former NFL players. Many were current pros in the Arena Football League. I was good, but I was not at their level. The casting director, aka "Coach," looked like he wanted to cut me multiple times. At the end of each day, he would read the numbers on the jerseys of the guys who'd made it to the next day and each day, for some reason, my number was read. The longer I lasted, the more determined I became to make it. What I didn't know until years later was the story I mentioned earlier: the casting director's assistant, a woman named Amy whom I knew from my SlamBall days, was going to bat for me behind the scenes. Every time the coach went to cut me, she stopped him.

"This is the guy you want," Amy told him. "I promise you; he's going to be great."

"But check out his times in the forty," the guy replied. "He's not fast enough. Not big enough, either."

"Doesn't matter. Look, here are his SlamBall highlights. Watch this and you'll see what he's capable of physically. But even better, I know the kind of person he is. He'll be on time, he'll follow directions, he'll work his ass off every day. He's going to be phenomenal."

"Okay, if you want him, I'll take him . . . but you're putting your job on the line vouching for this guy. If he screws up . . ."

"He won't. You'll thank me later."

The coach came and told me that I'd made the cut for the prison football scenes that would be filmed over a three-month period in Santa Fe, New Mexico. I was a big ugly guy who looked like an inmate (and, unfortunately, had actual inmate experience thanks to my arrest in college), so picking me made sense. He went on to say that when the production returned to LA to shoot the movie's climax—the actual football game between the inmates and the guards—I would be replaced by "a better player." Fair enough, I thought. I was just thrilled to land a role no matter how small or temporary it might be.

A SPLIT-SECOND DECISION

About a month into production of *The Longest Yard* we were preparing to shoot the scene of the first time the prison inmates go onto the practice field together. You might remember this from the introduction. Once on the field the director told us to imagine that we'd just been released from our cells for the first time in a long time, and we were like a pack of wild animals . . . maniacs. For the highlight of this scene, Adam Sandler, who was reprising Burt Reynolds's starring role in the original movie, was supposed to take his place behind center to receive a snap. The center would hike the ball and it would shoot between Sandler's legs. Sandler would run back to get it and when he turned around to complete the play, all the inmates from both teams would be fighting each other. As we rehearsed this scene the stunt coordinator was on the field pairing people up, offense versus defense. "You two guys fight each other over here, you three over there," etc. We were told to throw each other around and duke it out and just have some rowdy fun with it. The plan was to film the scene, review the tape, and see what worked and what didn't work.

I was a defensive player at the safety position out in the center of the field by myself. The stunt coordinator hadn't told me what to do, so I spoke up.

"Excuse me, sir," I called out. "There's nobody close to me. What should I do?"

He looked around for a moment and pointed down field.

"Run over there to the receiver and the cornerback and mix it up with them."

"Okay, got it."

It just so happened that the guys playing the cornerback and receiver were friends of mine (again, we were all good friends by this point), so I tried to think of something crazy to do to them when I got down there. Suddenly the director yelled "Action!" and the cameras started rolling. Still not knowing how I was going to "mix it up with them" specifically, I took off running full blast toward my targets who were already shoving each other around while they waited for me to join them. And then it hit me: *Drop kick both of them at the same time!*

So that's what I did. I took a deep breath and at precisely the right moment jumped up and kicked both guys squarely in their chests. They went down like lead weights and of course, so did I. The three of us landed in a heap and rolled around on the ground wrestling and punching each other until we heard, "Cut!"

While we inmates caught our collective breath and stood on the field chattering and laughing about how much fun that was, Sandler and the directors went into the production tent to look at the replays of the various camera angles on the monitors. They were in there a couple of minutes when suddenly the whole tent erupted in whoops and shouts. Then I heard it:

"Who drop kicked somebody?!?!?" was shouted enthusiastically from the tent.

My friends on either side of me froze and looked at me with eyes wide. *Oh man. I shouldn't have done that . . . I went too far with the drop kick. I am SO fired.* I tried to make myself invisible behind my buddies.

The stunt coordinator emerged from the tent and yelled, "Who did that drop kick?"

There was no point trying to hide. They'd figure out it was me eventually because the whole thing was caught on tape. I stepped out from behind my teammates.

"Um, that was me, sir," I said. "I thought it would be funny. I'm sorry."

"Sorry? It was awesome! Line up and get ready to do it again, we're setting up a camera to focus on it this take."

That's the story of my first real stunt in Hollywood, something I made up on the fly and thought I got fired for. Thanks to that drop kick, and my all-around play and character, the football coordinator changed his mind about replacing me with "a better player" for the remainder of the movie. He kept me on. Back in LA, as we prepared to film the opening kickoff of the big game, the director came to me and asked if I could do the drop kick again.

"Absolutely I can kick them again!" I said.

The drop kick I did that day not only made it into the movie but also the trailer shown all around the world to promote the film. I made more money during those four months on *The Longest Yard* than I made in an entire year of teaching. I moved off of Chris's sofa and into my own apartment by the beach.

INSIGHT AND STORIES FROM *THE LONGEST YARD*

The three months in Santa Fe were indescribably fun and rewarding. Much like my SlamBall days, I found myself surrounded by yet another group of awesome guys who were down-to-earth, funny people, and superior athletes. We all became great friends. During the day we'd play football for the movie, on our days off we hit the gym together, and at night we'd all go out. On this particular movie there was no separation between us and the big-name actors because they were on the football team with us. They had to practice with us every day and learn all the plays just like we did.

The cast camaraderie even spilled over after the workday was done. Adam Sandler and the director ate dinner with us much of the time, and every Monday after work we'd go to a bar to watch *Monday Night Football.* I remember one time it was me, another stunt guy, Adam, and two of his buddies sitting at a table in that bar. As I sat there across from Adam, it dawned on me that this was a pretty insane life I was living. I was hanging out with one of Hollywood's biggest stars and he was treating me like a friend. It was cool and weird at the same time. He was a normal, decent, likeable guy . . . the opposite of the way most people imagine celebrities to be.

I have a story about Adam that illustrates my point. As often happens in movies, some people are on the project from start to finish and others come and go throughout the shoot. One of the guys who was hired for *The Longest Yard* for only a few weeks asked me if he thought it'd be okay to talk to Adam. I informed him that Adam has been "one of the guys" since day one and as long as you treat him as such you can talk to him whenever he's around. Well, about an hour later I and some of the football guys were killing time on set between shots and Adam joined our little circle of conversation, as he often did. Very casually that same guy who had only been working for a few days asked Adam if he knew of any dinner spots around town that he would recommend, someplace nice but not too fancy, where he could take his wife. He was from somewhere in the Midwest, I think, and hadn't been out to California before so he'd brought his wife along to make a little vacation out of his job. Adam recommended a restaurant that he thought would be perfect, explaining that it was on the beach, had excellent food, and was not too expensive. The guy thanked Adam and we went back to our normal conversation about football or whatever it was we were talking about.

At the end of the day Adam's assistant tracked this guy down and asked if he still wanted reservations at that dinner spot. He was taken aback but said, "Yeah, absolutely. Thank you very much." The guy and his wife went to dinner that night at the place Adam recommended, and it was perfect—just what he was looking for. He was still in awe that Adam went so far as to get him reservations, but the surprises didn't stop there. When the bill came, he saw that it was paid in full. Adam had picked up the tab.

That's the type of person Adam Sandler is and that says more about him than any level of fame or fortune he has acquired. If I never see him again, that's a person I will remember and speak fondly of for the remainder of my life.

And then there was Burt Reynolds, another great guy. He had a soft spot for stuntmen because he started out in show business as a stuntman himself. He treated all of us stunt guys like old friends and loved to tell us stories about the crazy things that had happened to him over the course of his life.

He treated everybody so well, as did Sandler and the rest of the big-name performers. I couldn't have asked for a better group of actors for my first movie. I wasn't yet sure I belonged in their world, but they tried hard to make me feel as if I did. I was—and I remain—so grateful to them for their warm welcome into the movie industry.

NOW WHAT?!?

After *The Longest Yard* ended, I found myself in that familiar space of in between. This time it felt different, though. It was filled with hope and excitement for the future instead of stress and despair about next month's bills. I stayed in touch with Chris and Dustin and some of the other stuntmen I'd met hoping for leads. Nothing came right away. I learned that jobs in "the industry" were often spread out by months if you were even lucky enough to get another one. Especially when you are first starting. I went back to doing odd jobs like bartending, security work, giving private baseball lessons; anything I could scrounge up to stay afloat while I figured out the path to more movies. I was back in the in between but this time there was a plan, I was in LA, I had a few bucks in the bank, was debt free, and had a tangible career to aspire to. Finding good paying odd jobs that were possible to leave when a movie called wasn't tough in LA as everyone is trying to make it in the business and the support economy knows that.

It was at one of those odd jobs that I had a seemingly benign conversation with a friend that I've always remembered. I had just finished giving a personal training session when another personal trainer and friend of mine sat down beside me while we waited for our next clients to arrive.

We were bitching about how hard it is to survive in LA doing part-time work when he turned to me and said decisively, "In five years I'm going to own my own gym on the beach somewhere. Where do you see yourself in five years, Cass?"

I didn't hesitate for a second.

"That's easy," I replied. "Five years from now I'll be doing stunts in some of this town's biggest movies. I'll have so many movies lined up, I won't have time for anything else, and I'll never have to worry about how to pay my bills again."

Sure enough, five years later my friend had his own gym on the beach, and I was no longer working part-time jobs and had become an established Hollywood stuntman. Those five years were not easy and involved a commitment to a goal and taking small steps every day toward that goal.

10

THE WILL TO W.I.N.

The fight is won or lost far away from witnesses—behind the lines, in the gym, and out there on the road, long before I dance under those lights.

—MUHAMMAD ALI

WHETHER IT'S LOSING WEIGHT, being debt free, making the winning shot in the big game, attracting the perfect mate, or landing a dream job, most of us can easily identify a few personal goals. The trick is figuring out how to go from Dreamer to Achiever. How do you turn that lofty goal into a reality? How do you climb a mountain that's so high you can't even see the summit from where you're standing today?

This was the dilemma I faced as I set out to make a name for myself in the stunt world. Dreaming of being an elite Hollywood stuntman is a piece of cake . . . anyone can do it and in fact, countless people do. The difference between them and me is that I figured out what I had to do to make it happen, and I did it. Sounds simple, right? But ask yourself this: If it's so simple, why don't more of us do it? Why do so many people get permanently stuck in wishful-thinking mode and never attain the goals they've set for themselves?

I believe it's because they focus on the future rather than the present moment. They put their attention on *the result*, not on *how to get* the result. It's a subtle but powerful distinction. If you're lying there dreaming of making the winning touchdown in the big game, you're wasting time that could be spent working on one of the skills it takes to make touchdowns. It's about breaking your goals into steps . . . and not just normal steps but tiny, bite-sized pieces. I'm talking *miniscule steps*, and they have to be steps that can be taken *right now*. That's the key.

The person who explained this concept the best was Lou Holtz, one of the winningest college football coaches of all time. The reason his teams at the University of Notre Dame won so many games was because he taught them a simple formula for staying laser-focused on the power of the present moment. He called this formula **W.I.N.**, or **W**hat's **I**mportant **N**OW? Here's how it works. Instead of thinking about the future (the upcoming game) or the past (mistakes; past victories or losses), Holtz instructed his players to check in with themselves multiple times every day, both on and off the field, and say to themselves, "**W.I.N. W**hat's **I**mportant **N**OW?" If it's first thing in the morning, the answer to that question might be, "Fuel my body with a big healthy breakfast." After that it might be, "Pay attention in class so I can keep my scholarship." That afternoon at the gym, "Do one more set of squats than I did last time." As he's suiting up for practice, "Lace up my cleats properly so I don't get blisters." During drills, "Break through this line!" After dinner, "Study my playbook." That night, "Get a solid eight hours' sleep."

By the end of the day, thanks to the **W.I.N.** question, that young man and every one of his teammates will have taken dozens and dozens of steps toward their goal. Can you see how that simple shift in focus moves the needle? How easily it takes you from Dreamer to Achiever?

This is how I went from being a wannabe in Hollywood to earning the coveted title of "stuntman." The stunt world is extremely competitive. Breaking into it was a battle I won by taking one tiny step at a time and remembering Who I am when the going got rough. The grind it took to get to have a career as a stuntman was a long and hard-fought one that was frustrating at times. Whenever I felt overwhelmed by how far I had to go, I'd ask myself "**W**hat's **I**mportant **N**OW?" and take that one tiny step forward.

W.I.N.

WHAT'S IMPORTANT NOW?

THE ONLY INVESTMENT THAT CAN'T LOSE VALUE

Much like I'd done back in junior high when I stopped talking and observed my classmates for clues about how to get along, I quietly evaluated the stunt landscape to gain a deeper understanding of the industry and my potential role in it. I saw that in the stunt world, everyone starts at the bottom and only the hardest workers climb their way up over time. Of course, there are a few exceptions. Someone might have an advantage due to their family name and one or two lucky guys might fall into a big job right away and never look back, but everyone else had a hard grind to become successful. In fact, I refused to call myself a stuntman for years until I felt I had enough experience and a good enough reputation, because I knew what real stunt people were doing every day, and for a long time I wasn't on that level. I was determined to get there though, so I made a commitment to invest in myself and do whatever it took to become the best I could be.

In my analysis of the stunt world, I saw that getting the most lucrative work was about word of mouth, gaining experience, building a reputation, networking, training with the right people, and learning specific skills, so I set about doing all of those things. Even if a job required me to work for free, I took it. I did fight training. I traveled hours away from home to get face time with experts to learn certain skills and paid a lot of money for specialized classes like stunt driving—all out of pocket. I played in the stuntman softball league, went to the stuntman golf tournaments, engaged in every aspect of the stunt community. That was how I spent my time while I waited for the next gig to come along.

While on this grind, my friend Justin let me know that there was a tryout coming up for a new football movie, *Gridiron Gang* staring Dwayne Johnson, aka The Rock. As luck would have it, Justin was the one hiring the football talent for this picture. He was also heavily involved in SlamBall and was one of the people who ran the tryout in Philly and whom I had interacted with regularly during the season. He was also good friends with Chris and his roommates and got his start in the movie business by doing football stuntwork with them—most famously years earlier on the Keanu Reeves movie *The Replacements.* I showed up to the interview portion of the audition just like I did at the one for *The Longest Yard* and there was Justin sitting at the table. When it was my turn to interview, I stepped up and said hello. He looked at me quizzically.

"What are you doing here?" he asked.

"What do you mean, 'what am I doing here?'" I replied. "I want to be in the movie!"

"Well yeah, but you don't have to do the interview. I know you. Just come back tomorrow for the tryout."

I shrugged and did what I was told. I showed up at the tryout the next day ready to go, ready to prove myself. Justin walked up to me and said, "Go sit over there, Cass. You don't have to do any of this. You're in."

To be honest I felt a bit guilty watching players bust their ass like I did during *The Longest Yard* tryout while I pretty much just hung out. But ultimately SlamBall, my continuous grind in the stunt community, and my performance in *The Longest Yard* all served as my tryout so there was no more need for Justin to evaluate my talent. Like he said, I was in.

Shooting for *Gridiron Gang* was in Malibu, about a two-hour drive from my home. I had to be on the road by five a.m. every morning to make it to the set on time, but that was fine with me. I had a job and that was all that mattered. A lot of the same guys from *The Longest Yard* were also in this movie so it was like a big family reunion.

I also made a couple of new friends on that set: two brothers, both who'd played college football and one who had gone on to the NFL. Their stepfather was a legend in the stunt world, who had appeared in multiple Oscar-winning movies. When I learned that he was my new friends' stepdad, I was shocked. If they had that kind of legacy, why were they doing the same low-level job I was doing? Movies have a hierarchy of pay and prestige. And though I was very happy doing this football work, at the end of the day it was the bottom of the barrel for legit stunt people. Why weren't they automatically elevated to the bigger shows and better paying gigs? As I got to know them and their family better, I learned the answer. The old man intentionally cut his stepsons no slack. He told them that if they wanted to get into the movie business, they would have to earn their way just like he had . . . just like everyone else. He made them do the grunt work, and as a result they were the most humble, talented people around. They moved up the ranks on their own merits not because of their most impressive Whats but because of their most impressive Who. My association with this family would benefit me immensely, not because they helped me land jobs but because they were awesome role models and encouragers. They introduced me to the next level of the business and were always happy to give me advice and vouch for me when they could.

The moral of the story: *you never know who you may be networking with even when you think you're just hanging out with friends. Behave accordingly!* Surround yourself with good people, and when you can, with good people who are where you want to be. However, don't pick these people because of What they are. Just like you shouldn't value your What over your Who, you shouldn't value anyone else this way either.

BREAKING THROUGH

For the first five years in LA my life went something like this: be broke, do a football movie, be an extra on a commercial, have some money, be broke, do some personal training, be broke, tend bar, get another commercial . . . all the while doing whatever I could to build my skills, my network, and my reputation. Those last two, network and reputation, turned out to be much more important than I realized initially. It was an eye-opener to see just how different this world was from anything I'd encountered in the past. As an athlete my experience had been that if you're talented enough, you'll play. But in the stunt world, virtually EVERYONE is talented. You can't just sit there and wait for the powers-that-be to recognize your skills. You have to sell yourself and literally tell them how good you are. That's not my style; besides, I could see with my own eyes that the people who sold themselves like that didn't necessarily build careers . . . they just got jobs. Two vastly different things. My reluctance to toot my own horn definitely slowed my progress in the movie business, but I believed it was smarter to play the long game, build relationships, and work toward having a lasting career rather than sing my own praises and risk not being able to live up to the hype.

My strategy paid off. By the end of those five long hard years, I was getting plenty of movie roles as a legit stuntman. I kept my head down, continued asking myself "**W**hat's **I**mportant **N**ow?" and kept on doing whatever I had to do to keep moving forward.

Among the many TV shows were *Friday Night Lights*, *Sons of Anarchy*, *CSI: Crime Scene Investigation*, *Punk'd*, and *Late Night with Conan O'Brien*. I was hired to train superstar performers for stunts in their music videos and commercials, including choreographing and teaching Nicki Minaj how to fight ninjas for a music video, and teaching Justin Bieber how to fly on wires for a TV commercial for his cologne. I was also performing stunts on some of the biggest video games in the world like *Halo*, *Gears of War*, and *NFL Madden*.

Performing motion capture for the NFL Madden *video game*

And then there were the movies: *Salt*, *Transformers*, *The Hunger Games: Mockingjay I* and *II*, *Ant-Man*, *I Am Number Four*, *Captain America*, *Guardians of the Galaxy*, *Spider-Man*, *Black Panther*, *The Dark Knight Rises*, and many, many more.

This is the ride I was on. It was as if one day I looked up and discovered that I was all in. It was during the filming of *The Dark Knight Rises* that I realized just how far I'd come in the business. I was on the set as part of the stunt team, hired to be one of the football players in the scene where the field blows up. I was hired by the legit stunt coordinator, not the football coordinator—an important distinction in the business. I was on the stunt team that did the fights, cars, and fire . . . the top of the barrel and no longer on the team that only did the football work. On my first day I changed my clothes in the same locker room as the regular football players while filming the climactic stadium scene. The same type of locker room I was in during *The Longest Yard* and *Gridiron Gang*, with the same type of people. This was a new, younger wave of athletes that eventually wanted to get where I was if they decided to stay in the business. Although I'd been out of the football movie world for a while, I recognized a few of the guys in that locker room, most notably the movie's football coordinator, aka "Coach." It was the same football coordinator from my first movie, *The Longest Yard* . . . the guy who wanted to cut me so many times during the tryout for that movie and who only let me on the team after his assistant vouched for me. When we saw each other, we hugged and caught up on old times. We talked about when I was a grunt extra scraping and clawing for jobs, making a couple hundred bucks a day at best. After a few minutes of chatting, he gathered his football players around and introduced me to them.

"Guys, a few years ago Cass was doing the exact same thing you're doing today," he told them. "He started out cleats-on-the-field, just like you. But now he's working on legit stunt teams making the big money, earning residuals, being flown all over the country for work in some of the highest-budget movies in the industry. He's a real-world example of how far you can go in Hollywood with the right work ethic, determination, and grit. Remember that when you're out on the field today."

As I looked around the locker room at those guys who were working so hard and dreaming so big, I felt incredibly humbled and grateful. Although I was hardly an overnight sensation, I had made it. I had leveraged my talents to do work I enjoyed with people I respected, and I was finally earning a comfortable living. I was happy with my What and my Who . . . and whenever you can bring those two elements into alignment, it's golden. I felt great about myself and the direction I was headed. I was proud of my What, as it was a hard-fought right to be called a stuntman, but I wasn't enamored by it. My Who was still steering the Ship of Kevin, but for once all the planks seemed in great working order.

"NEW MEGAN," PLUS THREE

When I was working on my stunt career I lived in Hermosa Beach, a town on the western edge of the LA metro area. I dated a bit during that time but not a lot; I was essentially consumed with building my career and enjoying the beach life. I knew that I couldn't make someone else happy until I was satisfied with myself. I wasn't letting anyone else on my leaking ship. But when I felt it was strong enough to support the weight, I opened myself up to the idea of building a crew.

Hermosa Beach is a small town, and if you're there long enough you'll run into the same people time and again. Such was the case with me and a pretty girl named Megan. When she and I first met she was finishing up her undergrad work at the University of Southern California. We had some mutual friends; guys I did football movies with who played at USC as well as some other shared beach buddies. For that reason, I kept bumping into her everywhere I went. Megan and I were slightly more than acquaintances for a few years then became friends as our individual peer groups started to gravitate toward each other. We would see each other at the beach and at all the same parties. She was even at my thirtieth birthday party with her then-significant other and became good friends with my then-girlfriend, another Meghan who spelled her name with an "h."

At some point both Megan and I found ourselves single simultaneously. Timing is everything, they say. I asked her out, she accepted, and the deal was essentially done. We quickly discovered that our personalities and values were a good match. I was crazy about her. When I told my family about her, they christened her "New Megan" to distinguish her from "Old Meghan."

New Megan and I talked a lot about how tired we were of the Peter Pan mentality of Southern California and how we both wanted to move back to the East Coast eventually to be closer to our families. She worked for a company that allowed her to telecommute, so as long as she was close to an airport to travel a few times a month, she could live anywhere. At the same time, the movie business had significantly reduced the amount of filming they were doing in and around LA, so I was working on projects all across the country. I could live anywhere I wanted as well. We got married and moved to North Carolina. Mom and my uncles were thrilled. They liked Megan a lot and loved having us close by. During our first Christmas as a married couple we found more than one present under the tree addressed to "New Megan."

Within a couple of years Megan and I went from "couple" to "family" thanks to the arrival of our daughter, Victoria. Like most things in my life, she didn't come easy. We tried for a while to get pregnant but weren't having any luck. After a miscarriage and a few doctor visits we learned that Megan had a minor physical issue that would make it tough for us to conceive. However, we were perfect candidates for in vitro fertilization (IVF). Throughout this experience my wife had to be the strong and perseverant one and I was stuck in a supporting role. I found myself in unfamiliar territory again. Typically, I was dealing with my own problems that I could work on myself where only I would be responsible for the outcome. I was involved in this problem, but it wasn't mine alone and it certainly wasn't mine physically. Being able to take a back seat and support my wife through this was very humbling. She was a rock star. She even started a private Facebook page to help other women going through the same process where she outlined the entire experience; the ups, downs, and everything in-between. When Victoria finally arrived, she was perfect. Awkwardly perfect. Nobody could believe she was our baby. She was too cute and way too easygoing. We were spoiled with her from Day One.

Eighteen months later karma would come a' knockin'. We were able to conceive naturally fairly quickly after Victoria was born and soon had the baby everyone expected we would. Wild, happy, crazy, strong, and full of piss and vinegar: another daughter, this one named Blake. A chip off the old block, apparently. Like my mom said recently, "She's tough like her daddy . . . she stumbles and tumbles and jumps up smiling!"

Somehow, hearing that, everything in my life suddenly made sense. We didn't stop there, and a little over two years after Blake was born came another girl, Rae. The first half of my life seemed to harden me emotionally as well as physically at every turn. Now it looks like the second half, with three daughters, is going to be busy softening me up. I'm hoping to find that sweet spot in the middle.

SAILING INTO HOME PORT

I seem to have run in a great circle, and met
myself again on the starting line.

—JEANETTE WINTERSON

THERE YOU HAVE IT . . . my understanding of my life so far. As I've looked back on my personal history while writing this book, I've felt good about the things I've done and how far I've come. If someone had told ten-year-old Rat Boy that he would grow up to be in movies like *Spider-Man* and *Guardians of the Galaxy* someday, he would not have believed it. To be honest, I still have to pinch myself sometimes. If I was going to fall into a career, I'm really happy it was something as interesting, fun, and challenging as being a stuntman. That I managed to overcome so many obstacles to get there (and beyond) is pretty amazing to me.

I'm also struck by the realization that at my core I am essentially the same person I've always been. Just a little older, hopefully a lot wiser, and even more settled in my conviction that it's not What we are but Who we are that matters most. As various planks have fallen from the Ship of Kevin over the years, the one thing that sustained me was the confidence that I could rebuild, retake the helm, and sail in a new direction.

IT'S NOT WHAT WE ARE BUT WHO WE ARE THAT MATTERS MOST.

In fact, I'm doing that very thing right now. This time it's not because I have to, but because I want to. It would be easy for me to keep being a stuntman, making good money and having cool stories to tell. But since I've never taken much stock in *What* I am, I'm listening to an internal stirring that's telling me to do more . . . to find a way to have a positive influence on people's lives. It's the same internal stirring that compelled me to major in education and be a teacher in Baltimore. Ever since my college days I've dreamed of having my own indoor sports facility. I envision running camps for kids where they could learn not only athletic skills but also the kinds of life skills I've highlighted in this book. Kids from the inner city, rich kids, poor kids, rural kids . . . all kids could benefit from learning about the Who vs. What questions and The Ship of Theseus Paradox while at the same time gaining self-confidence through participation in sports.

My dream is to have motivational speakers come into my facility and inspire kids in ways that transcend athletics. I imagine hiring high school and college athletes, some of whom might be having issues in their own life transitions, to come in and teach and mentor the younger ones, which would increase the older ones' confidence as well. I even went so far as to write business plans for a place like this, but I never followed through on it. Until now.

As I write this I'm shopping for the right space in Charlotte, North Carolina, where my coaching and teaching dream will finally become a reality. Rather than focusing on the mainstream sports, I intend to carve out a different niche. During my stunt career I've had the pleasure of working alongside many pro athletes: cowboys, UFC fighters, Cirque du Soleil performers, *X Games* champions, martial artists, and of course football players. To say I learned a lot from these people would be an understatement. I was introduced to these worlds and the people who come from them in an up-close and personal way through stunt work. Being surrounded by, befriending, and competing for jobs with people from so many different backgrounds (Whats) was very interesting. But even more interesting was the fact that the ones who made it to the top of the business were the ones most grounded in their Who. In a sea where everyone had an impressive What, your character, work ethic, honesty, and personality were the differentiators. The things I took away from these experiences shined the light on what kind of business I want to be a part of moving forward. Over and over again, the people I met from the cowboy world or the X Games world (motocross, skateboarding, skydiving, parkour, BMX, etc.) had the strongest Who. Of course, there were exceptions like my two football friends and others, but time and time again the guys from these backgrounds had a grip on that Who vs. What balance. Because of that they were and will continue to be very successful in stunts and life in general. This pointed my focus as a businessman toward this world. I want to impart this kind of balance on the next generation. I am opening an *American Ninja Warrior*–type facility. I have partnered with a company called Ninja Nation to bring two or three franchise locations to the Charlotte area.

Forged through training, competition, and challenge, this environment can help kids of all ability levels find that balance of confidence and humility that is so important in this world. Exposure to this kind of healthy mindset will be super beneficial to the children lucky enough to experience it. Positive energy builds confidence in the right way, even more than mainstream sports do, in my opinion. There are definitely a lot of positive attributes to playing football, baseball, and basketball, but you have to be at a certain ability level to capture them, and by the time you get there people are already talking about college scholarships. That's happening at an alarmingly young age nowadays. Improving simply for the sake of improving, challenging yourself just for the high of achieving a goal, and the positive impact that has on kids is invaluable. I think kids will have a better chance of not taking themselves too seriously in the environment I'm creating and not getting bogged down with playing sports just to earn a scholarship or make it to the big leagues someday . . . things that may or may not happen. Who knows, maybe some of the kids who train at my facility will grow up to have wonderful stunt careers in Hollywood, just as I've had.

Regardless of how far they take their involvement in sports, I want them to come away from my facility feeling great about themselves. Humble, quiet confidence is what we're aiming for because once they have that, they will carry that positivity into every aspect of their lives.

> Your confidence as a baseball player, swimmer, or parkour athlete (or any endeavor you enjoy) helps you be confident as a friend, which helps you be confident as a student, which helps you be confident as a worker, a neighbor, a partner, and a parent, which helps you be a confident citizen of the world.

Confidence in a What can strengthen your Who. Transferring that confidence to your Who so you can tap into it in any environment is the challenge. When you have that kind of strength, people will see it and treat you accordingly. A Who constructed from positive intangibles like confidence, humility, integrity, grit, determination, and dependability will keep your ship afloat better than all the planks, masts, and sails in the boatyard. I know from experience that the What that gets you through one storm at sea won't always get you through the next one. Baseball sustained me through the trials of junior high, but it couldn't get me through anything I go through today as a family man and entrepreneur. For that I'll have to rely on something bigger, deeper, and more powerful. Something that was strengthened and built in part on the baseball field, but that doesn't exist on that field alone. With knowledge of Who I am, I'm confident that I will not simply get past the challenges that lie ahead, *I will conquer them.*

How about you? Think back to the beginning of this book when I first brought up the What vs. Who questions and asked for your thoughts on The Ship of Theseus Paradox. If I asked you those same questions today, would your answers have changed? Do you know Who and What you are at this point in your life? Whether you do or don't, I want you to promise me these three things:

1. That you'll check in with yourself and think about these questions often, for the rest of your life;
2. That you'll spread this philosophy to the people around you—especially the younger ones; and
3. That you'll make the conscious decision to be grounded in your Who, not your What.

By doing these three things, your self-knowledge will grow and your confidence will soar. No matter how many planks need to be replaced on your Ship, you'll be able to do it with the least amount of time drifting aimlessly at sea . . . you'll be resilient in a way that everyone around you will want to know how you do it! You'll learn to reinvent yourself whenever you need to, viewing transitions not as anxiety-ridden catastrophes but exciting, invigorating challenges (and maybe even gifts). You'll have a stronger sense of your place in the world and how you can contribute to making the world better. You'll never allow anyone to pigeonhole you or diminish your value as a human being. You'll become the best, most courageous version of yourself that you can possibly be. If you can do that, I would consider it a major win . . . not just for you, but for every person whose life you will touch.

AUTHOR Q&A

1. **What do you hope readers take away from this book?**

   I hope that readers learn that their lives will be ongoing and constant adjustments. Be comfortable in that process. Everyone has something to be confident about, as well as the ability to be humble. Combining those two qualities will get you through the many transitions in life. Don't fall in love with who you were yesterday, as that person may hold you back tomorrow.

2. **If you hadn't constantly replaced planks in your life and had accepted that you were just the "Deformed Bullied Kid," how do you think your life would have been different?**

   I can't see how attaching your self-worth to a negative perception held by others could ever result in any kind of success or happiness. So yes, my life would've been very different had I not had the fortitude to look internally and not externally and replace planks to build myself up. I would have either been very egotistical or very depressed—maybe both. I for sure wouldn't have been able to form strong, lasting friendships with so many great people had I not changed my self-perception. Depression is at an all-time high right now, and this attachment to external perceptions and the inability to look inside and replace planks is likely a huge factor contributing to this.

3. **Do you think everyone can turn negatives into positives? What would you tell someone who thinks they're simply not able to do so? That the negative Whats are simply too overwhelming?**

   Absolutely everyone can turn negatives into positives. Or at the very least turn them neutral and not let those negatives hold them back. If a person feels their *What* is too overwhelming, it's only because they haven't built up their foundational *Who* yet. Focus on the little things that make you *you*, like kindness, work ethic, and honesty. Build foundational confidence on those traits, practice positive self-talk, and your definition of "overwhelming" will change quickly.

4. **If you could meet your younger self—the boy being bullied and often feeling alone and misunderstood at home—what would you say to him? Do you think he'd listen?**

   Future me would be the only person he would listen to—HA! I would say, "Stay the course, stay grounded in good friendships, but put more effort into building the family relationships. You never know how long they will be around."

5. **You are very candid about the bullying you experienced growing up. Even though you have such a positive attitude and takeaway now about what you learned from those incidents, what was it like for you to revisit so many difficult memories as you wrote this memoir?**

   I became friends with many of the kids who had bullied me a few years earlier, and so I didn't hold any grudges. I think that's why it wasn't too tough to mentally go back to those places. Now, realizing those instances were the root of much of my growth made me prouder of how I handled most of the bullying. Also, looking back as an adult, with experience teaching and coaching kids, it's even easier to find empathy for the bullies. They were going through their own battles I knew nothing about.

6. **You say that although you didn't enjoy being bullied, you also didn't internalize it to the point that it became your Who. In your view it was just another plank on the Ship of Kevin . . . a plank you could toss overboard when you didn't want to think about it anymore. Was that mindset something you always remember having or was it something you slowly learned growing up as the best way to cope? What advice can you give readers to embrace this mindset of seeing what could be a major obstacle as simply one plank of many that can be replaced?**

I think this mindset is the secret sauce I'm trying to deliver in this book. For me, it was present at such a young age due to my birth defect and speech impediment; I never knew anything different. Finding confidence in something internal is the key, no matter how small that thing is. Realizing that the external (speech and facial deformity included) is secondary to internal confidence allows you to replace planks with less stress. This can be accomplished at any age, but you must look inside yourself and take accountability to build that foundation. WIN—"What's Important Now"—is something I keep close to my heart. Try to stay focused on the small, individual planks that need to be replaced without thinking about the bigger ramifications that may be lingering. One plank at a time, slow and steady wins the race.

7. **Could you expand on your very important statement that "Having the freedom to fail is a very precious gift"? How do you feel your life would have been different had you not been given this freedom? How might your Who have changed?**

It would be hard to stay humble if you are protected from failure throughout life. Not being able to blame anyone else forces you to come to grips with yourself. I couldn't blame my speech or appearance on any external factor, so I had to deal with it internally for as long as I can remember. I was lucky in that respect. Without the freedom to fail, you rob an individual of the fulfillment of success. If

I had been protected and shielded from failure, I would have had a huge ego, and on the day failure inevitably finally found me, I would have lashed out at any and all external variables and had a tough time building myself back up. My happiness would have been revealed as a shallow mirage once reality came to visit. Who's to say how I would've handled it, but I know the person that preceded it would have been a shallow mirage as well.

8. **What would your advice be to readers at a crossroads in their lives who wish to make a positive impact on themselves and others?**

   Sounds cliché but just start with the small steps in the right direction and let the momentum build. "A journey of 1,000 miles begins with one small step." Especially if your goal and motivation is to help others. For me, this builds energy for the product, transition, or process much faster and leaves me more fulfilled. Even if you are not trying to make an impact, but are simply at a crossroads in your life, focusing energy on helping someone else rejuvenates your soul in a way that can energize you through transition. Help yourself by helping others. Simple but true.

9. **You share so much insight throughout the book, but if you could give only one piece of advice to someone wishing to find long-term success in life—both as a person and in their career—what would it be?**

   I would first have to define success with that person. It's very hard to find long-term success (maybe impossible) when that success is defined by external validations like money, job title, or relationship status. Long-term success is grounded in being satisfied with who you are. The other stuff is icing on the cake. True, enduring success starts within and works its way out into the world. You'll be chasing your tail if you try to find it the other way around.

10. **Is there anything you didn't have space to explore in this book?**

    Leadership and how building up your Who makes you a better leader. The correlation between humble confidence and being an effective leader is a big deal. I didn't think I could approach this subject without getting too deep into it and distracting from the other themes in the book. This may be a good follow-up book or discussion, especially now that I naturally find myself in leadership positions. I have been told I have an innate leadership quality that so many people strive for, and I think it comes naturally for me because of the many things outlined in this book. Something there worth exploring.

11. **You're working on opening an *American Ninja Warrior*–type facility for kids where they can feel great about themselves and grow humble confidence. What has been the hardest part about starting this venture, the most unexpected part, and the most rewarding?**

    In all honesty, COVID has been the hardest part. Navigating the buildout process and trying to time things right has proven tough. At the end of the day, you must make a call and stick with it, and that tests anyone's confidence. The good news about COVID was I had plenty of time to think through all aspects of owning a business, read books, and talk to friends with experience on the topic. Film production was shut down, so I wasn't working on set, and so I had plenty of time, which led to not having much surprise me during the process. There were many frustrations, but nothing completely unexpected. Of course, the most rewarding parts are watching the kids overcome challenges every day and seeing their confidence grow.

12. **You wrote that "Great people don't talk about themselves; other people will do that for them," and to illustrate that point, shared compelling stories about Nelly, Angelina Jolie, Adam Sandler, and other celebrities. Is there anyone else in your life—famous**

or not—that embodied that idea of greatness whom you didn't include in the book?

So many people embodied this characteristic in my life. I think I have always been drawn to this type of person. My good friend Chris Robbins—a SlamBall teammate, fellow stuntman, pastor, father, husband, and the man who performed my wedding ceremony—comes to mind. As does the now super-famous actor Tom Holland. Tom has such a genuine joy for life and exuberant spirit, it's ridiculous. Also, another fellow stuntman and good friend who was one of the first internet-famous Parkour athletes, Damien Walters, springs to mind. I worked with him for a few months before someone showed me videos of what he could do physically. It's superhuman but pales in comparison to the type of friend, husband, son, and father he is. I could go on and on about the people I've been lucky enough to know who inspired me to focus on my humble confidence.

ABOUT THE AUTHOR

To bear trials with a calm mind robs
misfortune of its strength and burden.

—SENECA

STUNTMAN KEVIN CASSIDY has been making movie goers' hearts beat faster since 2005, when he appeared in his first feature film, the remake of *The Longest Yard* starring Adam Sandler, Chris Rock, and Burt Reynolds. Since then, "Cass" has become known industry-wide for his hard-hitting action in major motion pictures like *Black Panther*, multiple *Spider-Man* and *Ant-Man* movies, *Guardians of the Galaxy, Vol. 2, Captain America: Civil War, Salt, The Hunger Games: Mockingjay 1* and *2, The Dark Knight Rises*, and many others. His television appearances include episodes of

Punk'd, Dexter, CSI, Friday Night Lights, Late Night with Conan O'Brien, and *Sons of Anarchy.* He has also done motion capture work for EA Sports' *Madden NFL, HALO, Gears of War,* and many other video games, and trained performers Nicki Minaj, Rhianna, Britney Spears, and Justin Bieber for specialized action in their music videos.

Prior to becoming a stuntman, Cass was a standout high school and college athlete who went on to play professional baseball and SlamBall (an extreme form of full-contact basketball), which was televised on Spike TV in the early 2000s. He also taught middle school outside Washington, D.C., before answering Hollywood's call.

Cass was born on Long Island, New York, in 1977 with a severe facial deformity that made him the target of intense bullying throughout his childhood, causing him to think deeply about matters of identity, self-assurance, and the way social roles are constructed. That experience, along with his lifelong dream of teaching and coaching young people, led him to bringing Ninja Nation to the Charlotte area. A place where kids will not only learn fun athletic skills but also become the recipients of Cass's real-world lessons in confidence, humility, poise, and teamwork.

Cass lives with his wife, Megan, and their daughters Victoria, Blake, and Rae in Charlotte, North Carolina, where they enjoy the nearby lake, golf courses, sports teams, year-round community events, and time with friends and family.

To contact Cass for information about speaking engagements
and his training facility, email KCassidyConnect@gmail.com.
You can also check out his website, KevinCass.com,
and follow him on @Twitter, @Instagram, and @Facebook.